Use this unique code to
unlock Volume 6 in the
Delight App

CODE: V6CXN37

A COLLEGE WOMEN'S STUDY

"DELIGHT YOURSELF IN THE LORD, AND HE WILL GIVE YOU THE DESIRES OF YOUR HEART."
PSALM 37:4

Delight Ministries
www.delightministries.com

Printed in the United States of America
First Printing: August 2018
Believers Press
ISBN: 978-0-9906825-7-8

TABLE OF CONTENTS

OUR MISSION

Our mission is to invite college women into Christ-centered community that fosters vulnerability and transforms stories.

WHO WE ARE

We are a college women's community that grows together, serves together, learns together, and does life together while chasing the heart of God.

WHAT WE DO

We provide college women with the tools and resources to launch, grow, and sustain Christ-centered communities on college campuses. We create curriculum that tells the real stories of college women chasing the heart of God.

OUR STORY

We here at Delight are big believers in stories. Stories that move and inspire, take our breath away, stop us in our tracks, and change us forever. Delight was created as a platform for college women to not only share their stories, but also as a place to allow God to write stories more beautiful than we could ever even fathom.

SO LET US TELL YOU THE STORY OF DELIGHT.

Two freshmen girls meet at Belmont University and become best friends. On the last day of freshman year the two girls go to dinner with another girl. Girls talk the whole time about how AWESOME God is. The three girls go home for summer. One girl works as a waitress. One girl goes to Alaska for a mission experience. Other girl sells knives. Girls return in the fall. Girls go to church together. On the way home waitress girl asks the other two girls if they want to start a Bible study. Other two girls say yes because they both had the same nudging over the summer. Girls meet in the bell tower on campus two weeks later on a Friday morning for "Bible study". Twenty other girls come. Girls name Bible study Delight. Delight girls cook dinner together, study the Word together, serve hot chocolate to the homeless together, love on refugee kids together, stand for freedom together, wash cars together, and learn to live more like Christ together. Nine months later girls have grown from three to just under one hundred. The three girls are amazed and bewildered at all that God has done in and through Delight.

That is the quick and simple version of the story behind Delight. This story isn't necessarily unique and exciting. In fact, you've probably heard plenty of stories just like it. By this point, you may even be bored reading this story and wondering why you bothered reading it in the first place.

What makes this story different is where the significance lies. You won't find it in the characters, the setting, the climax, the dialogue, or even the theme. This story isn't actually about the story at all. It's about the author. An author that could take three sophomoric, average, ordinary girls and write His own beautiful story through them. An author that led unworthy and undeserving girls to start a Bible study that would eventually grow into a nationwide ministry devoted to serving college women. This story is about the King of Kings and the Prince of Peace. God is the ultimate author, the ultimate visionary, and the ultimate dreamer. We are so honored to be the characters of this story, but are so thankful that we don't hold the pen in our hands. We leave the real storywriting to the greatest storyteller of all time.

"MAY YOU HAVE THE POWER TO UNDERSTAND, AS ALL GOD'S PEOPLE SHOULD, HOW WIDE, HOW LONG, HOW HIGH AND HOW DEEP HIS LOVE IS."

EPHESIANS 3:18

DEAR FRIENDS,

As you begin to read the stories in this book, our message to you is simple.

Look for God in each and every moment this semester. Ask Him what He might be trying to say to you. Thank Him when you hear His voice loud and clear. Stand firm in the things He is doing in your heart. Be immovable, unshakeable, and steadfast—beautiful moments with God await.

'But thanks be to God! He gives us the victory through our Lord Jesus Christ. Therefore, my dear brothers and sisters, stand firm. Let nothing move you. Always give yourselves fully to the work of the Lord, because you know that your labor in the Lord is not in vain."
1 Corinthians 15:57-58

Mackenzie Baker + MacKenzie Wilson
Co-Founders of Delight Ministries

LILY JOY

CAMERON

CAROLINE

GRACIE

KATIE

ANGEL

HANNAH

LAUREN

EMILY

INDIA

LILY JOY

EAST TENNESSEE STATE UNIVERSITY
SOCIOLOGY
RECENT GRADUATE

Looking Up

LETTING GOD'S PRESENCE RESHAPE YOUR PERSPECTIVE

"Sometimes what we want is deeper clarity, but what we need is deeper faith."
Ann Voskamp

"Hello! I'm calling because I'm graduating in a few months, and I don't know what to do with my life. . . [insert nervous laugh]. . . I talked to my advisor and she told me I should call you and set up an appointment because you can help me with my résumé and finding a job, and that would be awesome because I seriously have no idea what I'm doing. . . Anyways, if you could just give me a call back at 423-439-4450. . . Oh wait. That's your phone number. You know that one. Don't call that one. Anyways, call me back when you can! Thanks! Bye!"

I don't think I have ever been as mortified in my life as I was in that moment. My only saving grace was that I also forgot to tell them my name.

That was me eight months ago when I was headed into my final semester of school. I tell you this story not because it's uniquely embarrassing, but rather because I think these moments are fairly common. We all know what it feels like when stress and anxiety have gotten the best of us and we've done something we later regretted or were embarrassed about. These moments typically come in times of transition or change, especially at the beginning of a new year or semester.

"'For I know the plans I have for you,' declares the LORD, 'plans to prosper you and not to harm you, plans to give you hope and a future.'"
Jeremiah 29:11

The start of a new semester can be the most wonderful, whimsical, yet terrifying time of the year, and my humiliating phone call with the career exploration center was only the beginning. It never fails that every year, after the first week of school, I call my parents crying and panicking. The first week of my senior year was no exception. My heart was filled with anticipation, my bags were filled with school supply shopping lists, my room was filled with the smell of used books, and my bank account was utterly and completely empty.

I walked to class the first day repeating to myself my beginning-of-the-school-year mantra: I can do this, this year is going to be different, I am going to stay ahead in all of my classes—but it was abruptly shut down at the sight of the first syllabus, handed to me by my photojournalism professor. And then I got the next one, the one after that, the one after that, and the one after that.

The number of assignments, quizzes, exams, and group projects piled on top of one another, forming a mountain too steep to climb. I had flashbacks to high school when my trigonometry teacher suggested in front of the whole class that I should go to my much smarter big sister for tutoring. Needless to say, at this point my mantra was a faint memory. So I decided to do what I do best: make lists and spreadsheets to help me conquer the semester.

I spent the next week consumed in planning. I color-coded and wrote down every assignment and deadline. I overbought school supplies so that I would never be caught unprepared, and I sent an overly dramatic text to my parents telling them I loved them dearly but that they probably wouldn't hear from me for the next few months. I told them not to worry because I would always be safely in the library or a coffee shop studying and that maybe if I had time I would make an exception to come back for Thanksgiving. . . which was maybe overly dramatic considering I was a commuter student who lived at home.

"Have I not commanded you? Be strong and courageous. Do not be discouraged, for the LORD your God will be with you wherever you go."
Joshua 1:9

One day while reading for my applied sociological research class, I decided to take a little break and check Instagram stories just to make sure the outside world still existed. That's when I saw it—a photo of the most lovely window with the most glorious view. The window arched from floor to ceiling revealing a beautiful panorama of our campus. It showed an old gray building, large swaying trees, and a small fountain below. I had never seen such a wonderful study spot and decided right then and there: it would be mine.

I immediately texted my friend who posted the picture and asked her where I could find the window. She said I couldn't miss it because it was in the big room on the third floor of the library, but she was wrong. I had practically lived out of that room for the past three years. It was where I always studied when I was on campus, and there was no way I had missed that giant window.

The next day after my last class, I went to the library in search of this mystery study paradise. Knowing my friend was wrong about its location, I checked the fourth floor first, but the window wasn't there. Next I checked the second floor, but still there was no window. Finally, laughing to myself at the absurdity of the thought of it being in my study room, I decided to check the third floor.

When I got to the third floor I turned left, passed the elevators, and walked into the large, silent study room which had been my solitude for the last three years. I looked up, turned my head to the right—and there was my window.

I stood silently in the doorway, mouth hanging open in shock. I flashed back through all of the days I spent rushing into this very room and turning left toward the tables. All of the times my eyes had been glued to my phone checking due dates and test scores when all I needed to do was look up. All of the hours I spent staring at a wall when I could have been looking out of that window. All this missed opportunity raced through my brain, and I began to cry.

I know it sounds crazy, crying at a window, but it was so much more than that. God had been taking me to this beautiful place for three years, and I had been too distracted and stuck in my own stressed-out, overwhelmed, and overworked world to notice.

I think this is exactly the reason why God doesn't tell us the plans he has for our lives. If Professor God gave us a syllabus charting out the course, we would become overwhelmed by what lies ahead. Some of us would drop out or stop trying, and others of us would start racing ahead trying to get to the finish line early. When we start treating our days like assignments to be completed, we stop seeing the beautiful moments God has placed before us.

"Light is sweet, and it pleases the eyes to see the sun."
Ecclesiastes 11:7

When we ignore His gifts, thinking our goals are better, we miss out on a chance to live a life of wonderful adventure with God. He doesn't call us to spend our days planning out every detail of our lives because at any moment, His plan could (and most likely will) alter everything we thought we knew. Living life with God means ending up somewhere totally different than where we expected to be.

I felt this happen so many times throughout college. I felt it when my boyfriend of three years broke up with me. I felt it when I was tested for polyps and didn't know if I would live past 22. I felt it when I realized I was being called to graduate early, start a Delight chapter, and abandon my plans to move across the country right after graduation. My time in college has taught me many things, but most importantly it has taught me to stop over-planning and simply trust in God to provide and guide. God asks us to constantly embrace whimsy and joy with Him, and accepting that offer is the only fully satisfying and perfectly wonderful way of life.

God doesn't tell us the plans He has for us because He doesn't want us enslaved by planning for our future, He wants us freely growing toward our future. When we choose to dwell in the presence of the Lord and allow Him to guide us and work through our lives, rather than being overwhelmed by the journey, we become astonished by His grace.

"I keep my eyes always on the LORD. With him at my right hand, I will not be shaken. Therefore my heart is glad and my tongue rejoices; my body also will rest secure, because you will not abandon me to the realm of the dead, nor will you let your faithful one see decay. You make known to me the path of life; you will fill me with joy in your presence, with eternal pleasures at your right hand."
Psalm 16:8-11

One of the most challenging parts of walking in faith is learning to let go and let God take the lead. It's difficult to embrace the knowledge that God's plan for us is so different from our own. We live with this constant struggle of wanting to understand why things didn't go according to our plans. I see this in myself when I look at past semesters and the overwhelming stress I had because I often find myself getting stuck on the why of it all. Why did God let me date a man who wasn't right for me for three years? Why did God not help me notice that window? Why didn't God stop me from leaving that embarrassing message?

This desire to understand God's plans isn't new—it dates way back to the Old Testament. The Lord told Abraham that his wife Sarah would bear a child in her old age, but after many years had passed and the Lord had not yet provided, they took matters into their own hands. Abraham had a child through Sarah's maidservant Hagar, creating conflict in their marriage. Again, the Lord went to Abraham and promised to provide a child for Sarah, but Sarah and Abraham laughed because they did not believe. Their unbelief proved foolish when Sarah, in her old age, bore a child named Isaac (meaning laughter).

We also see this need to understand God's plans when Habakkuk asks God why He is allowing the wicked to overpower the righteous in Judah. Though God acknowledges and agrees with Habakkuk, He still chooses not to intervene. God is looking at the long-term solutions to the problem whereas Habakkuk is blinded by the needs of the present moment. Sometimes God's solutions to the problems we're facing aren't what we would expect—because we wouldn't even consider them viable. His solutions may come at a completely different time in a completely different way than what we want, but they are always good. Habakkuk eventually learns to follow with praise, living a life full of prayer, knowing God will always prevail over evil and do right by His people.

I am constantly amazed at the parallels I find between the struggles in the Bible and the struggles in my own life. Like Abraham and Sarah, when I was shown a glimpse of my future I started relying on my own power rather than trusting God's ability and willingness to get me there. Abraham and Sarah laughed when they heard God's plan for their offspring because they didn't believe it would come to fruition, and similarly I am constantly laughing and telling myself "this is fine" when in reality I'm everything but fine. In those moments, I need to remember to turn to God before doing anything else. And like Habakkuk, I continually find that God's plans are incredibly different from my own, and I'm guessing you could say that about your life too. Rather than lying to ourselves and saying everything is fine when it's not, we need to learn to lift our praises and trust God's solutions as Habakkuk did. It's okay to be confused and unsure about God's plans, but the more often we practice accepting God's sovereignty over our lives, the easier it will become to give Him the reins.

Giving God control and accepting the truth that we know nothing about what will happen in our lives can be intimidating, especially if you're a big control freak with a love for lists and spreadsheets like me. Trusting

God includes letting Him take us down roads we never intended to travel and up mountains we never thought we would climb. The ironic thing is that even if we don't offer up control to God, He still has it. When we decide to let God take the lead in our lives, we find peace. Our spirits can finally rest in the knowledge that things will happen according to His plans and that His plans are far greater than our own. We can rest in knowing our lives will be lived perfectly through Him.

The Bible tells us that faith the size of a mustard seed can move mountains, but it's important to remember that our power doesn't move the mountains—God's power does. And even when we choose to walk with God, our lives will still have mountains. Even in the promised land there were walls to be torn down and sins to be forgiven. Each of us will still experience heavy moments, stressful semesters, and painful years, but when we put our faith in God instead of focusing on solving our problems, the trek becomes so much easier. Whether He moves your mountains or not, He'll be your hiking partner. And I don't know about you, but I'd rather hike up a mountain with God than stroll through a valley without Him any day.

"He replied, 'Because you have so little faith. Truly I tell you, if you have faith as small as a mustard seed, you can say to this mountain, "Move from here to there," and it will move. Nothing will be impossible for you.'"
Matthew 17:20

So as stressful as your semesters may be starting out, always remember that God wants you to lean into Him so He can give you the strength to pull through. Though it's important to have a plan and work toward your goals, it's also important to remember that God will change them and make them even better. Don't get so stuck in your expectations of the way things should be in the future that you miss out on the beauty of what is happening in the present. When we're locked on autopilot and focused on accomplishing our own plans, we overlook the giant windows of opportunity and precious moments which God has designed for us.

I overlooked my window for three years because I continually turned left instead of right, and I still think back to how blind I must have been to have missed it. How wonderful would it feel if rather than worrying with your head down, you chose to look up and found your window from God instead? I promise you, God has placed these windows in your life too. All you have to do is look up and follow Him.

Where do you feel God leading you to go? What window have you been missing because you've been turning left instead of right? One of the coolest things about God is that He loves us all so uniquely. Your window could be a friendship, a small group, a comforting book, or an awesome coffee shop. Whatever it is, God wants to lead you there.

That mortifying voicemail I left during my senior year now serves as a reminder of the life I was living before I started trusting God's plans for me. It was full of mistakes, my stress was evident, and I forgot about a lot of the important details. God has taken me to so many beautiful places since then. I have grown the most amazing friendships and created some of my most treasured memories. I have traveled, adventured, and explored like never before. I have discovered passions and dreams I never knew I had. God used me to bring people to the feet of Jesus. With God I have been filled with love and joy and emptied of worry and fear. Though there are miles to go on the mountains I'm climbing, I'm living my life with God as my hiking partner, and He never fails to point out the views.

Go hike up your mountain with God. Let Him guide you farther ahead, even when you feel sore and weak. Instead of looking at the path you think you should be on, look to where He walks instead. Let His grace overwhelm you. Feel the joy of His presence. Savor the journey, and enjoy the views.

"May the God of hope fill you with all joy and peace as you trust in him, so that you may overflow with hope by the power of the Holy Spirit."
Romans 15:13

KEY VERSES:
Jeremiah 29:11
Joshua 1:9
Ecclesiastes 11:7
Psalms 16:8-11
Matthew 17:20
Romans 15:13

DISCUSSION QUESTIONS:
+ Do times of transition or new beginnings leave you feeling
overwhelmed? How do stressful seasons affect the way you trust the
Lord?
+ In the Bible, Habakkuk chooses to lead a life of prayer and praise,
regardless of his circumstances. What are some practical ways you can
follow Habakkuk's example by living in prayer and praise while still
working your way up your mountains?
+ Lily Joy mentions that when we choose to dwell in God's presence we
become overwhelmed by His grace instead of being overwhelmed by the
journey. How have you been overwhelmed by your journey recently?
How might dwelling in God's presence reshape your perspective?
+ As you reflect on the last few months, what "windows" might you be
missing because you've been focused on your plans? What needs to
change in your life in order for you to see God's presence more clearly?
+ Has looking down left you too busy planning for your future that
you've missed opportunities to grow toward your future? What would it
look like today to stop planning and start growing?

DEVOTIONALS

CONTRIBUTOR: Whatley Hamilton

DAY 1

We tend to question God's plan for us in times of transition. We are faced with the unknown, the unexpected, and the unexplained. Frequently we plead with God to intervene and make clear for us the plan He has for us, or we try to force the imaginary plan we've created for ourselves. God has reasons for why He does not reveal the plans He has for our lives. Habakkuk experienced the struggle of desiring the knowledge behind God's plan for his life and for the world, but ultimately realized that the righteous live by faith.

Habakkuk lived during the final decade of the southern kingdom of Israel with the looming threat of a Babylonian invasion. He questions God's just rule over the world as he sees the injustices of a corrupt Judean society and God's proclamation of a Chaldean (Babylonian) invasion. He constantly struggles with understanding God's goodness during a time of abundant evil. Habakkuk laments to God to draw attention to injustice; yet, God responds with acknowledgement of the corruption in both Judea and Babylon. God will use these nations as catalysts to deliver justice to His people, even if God's plan is not to the liking of Habakkuk. Habakkuk's prayer in the final chapter of the book illustrates him pleading with God to act in the present, but he concludes with comprehending that trust and joy in God is more important than understanding God's actions and plans. It is an example of the righteous living by faith. Just as Habakkuk wrestles with the details of God's plan for justice, we must know that God is far too powerful and too great for us to know the reasons behind His plan. By living in prayer and praise, we learn to trust and find joy in God because His actions are just, good, sovereign, and perfect.

KEY VERSES:
"Though the fig tree does not bud and there are no grapes on the vines, though the olive crop fails and the fields produce no food, though there are no sheep in the pen and no cattle in the stalls, yet I will rejoice in the LORD, I will be joyful in God my Savior. The Sovereign LORD is my strength; he makes my feet like the feet of a deer, he enables me to tread on the heights."
Habakkuk 3:17-19

REFLECTION QUESTIONS:

+ Do times of transition or new beginnings leave you feeling overwhelmed? How do stressful seasons affect the way you trust the Lord?

+ In the Bible, Habakkuk chooses to lead a life of prayer and praise, regardless of his circumstances. What are some practical ways you can follow Habakkuk's example by living in prayer and praise while still working your way up your mountains?

DAY 2

Lily Joy writes that a reason why God doesn't reveal the plans He has for our lives is because we would be overwhelmed by them. Overwhelmed by His magnificent nature, glory, and power. While at times we are frustrated by not knowing the mysterious workings of God, He is purposeful in hiding them from our view, protecting us from drowning in a flood of knowledge.

We should take time to respect and admire God's decision to withhold His plans from us. God created every single aspect about each of us, knowing how we handle different situations, what makes us tick, and what makes us unique. As Christians, our relationship with God is intimate and personal. We strive to establish a deep spiritual connection with our Savior and consequently build trust in Him. As children obediently honor their father's decisions, we should honor God's wishes to withhold the plan He has for us.

Dwell in the truth that His plan is good, that He is in control, and that our individual wants and wishes are insignificant compared to His greater design. God is in control, and surrendering to His plan will yield overwhelming peace.

KEY VERSES:
"'For I know the plans I have for you,' declares the Lord, 'plans to prosper you and not to harm you, plans to give you hope and a future.'"
Jeremiah 29:11

"I keep my eyes always on the Lord. With him at my right hand, I will not be shaken. Therefore my heart is glad and my tongue rejoices; my body also will rest secure, because you will not abandon me to the realm of the dead, nor will you let your faithful one see decay. You make known to me the path of life; you will fill me with joy in your presence, with eternal pleasures at your right hand."
Psalms 16:8-11

REFLECTION QUESTIONS:
+ Lily Joy mentions that when we choose to dwell in God's presence we become overwhelmed by His grace instead of being overwhelmed by the journey. How have you been overwhelmed by your journey recently? How might dwelling in God's presence reshape your perspective?

DAY 3

We often are so focused on a specific path we have for ourselves that we neglect the opportunity to see spectacular God-given beauty. Maybe that opportunity is literally a lovely and cozy new study spot only several feet away from your typical study area like it was for Lily Joy, or maybe that opportunity is talking to the girl who's been sitting behind you in class all semester who came to the first Delight of the year but has yet to return. Even when the opportunities God gives to us are not explicit and bold, He has still masterly crafted when and where He reveals them to us.

Seize those little windows of opportunity through which God invites you to enter. Follow through on an opportunity God has given you, acknowledging all aspects of His greatness, power, and purpose. You never know where it will lead, but you can be sure God will be there with you. Let's practice surrendering ourselves to Him so that He can continue to shape and mold us into His trusting—and trustworthy—servants. As his children, we can speak with boldness and courage, empowered by the Holy Spirit to show God's greatness and help others believe. By noticing the windows of opportunity, we intentionally observe God working in our lives, helping us imitate and emulate Christ.

KEY VERSES:
"Light is sweet, and it pleases the eyes to see the sun."
Ecclesiastes 11:7

"May the God of hope fill you with all joy and peace as you trust in him, so that you may overflow with hope by the power of the Holy Spirit."
Romans 15:13

REFLECTION QUESTIONS:
+ As you reflect on the last few months, what "windows" might you be missing because you've been focused on your plans? What needs to change in your life in order for you to see God's presence more clearly?

When we focus too much on planning for the future, we lose our awe of God's wonders and mercies. At the same time, we begin to oversee our own personal plan for our lives instead of God's, reinforcing a belief that we have control and diminishing our trust in God's ability to guide us and provide for us.

We are supposed to find rest in God. In Genesis, we read about the way He ordered our planet with rhythm in mind—including a day of rest. God deemed rest as holy, as sacred. We live in a time and place where rest is compared to laziness, and we often feel pressure to actively seek and worship God all the time. It's honorable to want to actively celebrate God constantly, but we have to remind ourselves that the King has invited us to rest in Him—to seek peace and pursue it.

Take time to rest and marvel at His creation, to enjoy his splendor, and to renew your spirit. By constantly planning for the future, we have neglected the practice of resting. We cannot grow toward the future if we lose focus of our actual purpose. By halting our busyness, we can find rest in God and His plan to provide and guide us down the path He designed.

KEY VERSES:
"Have I not commanded you? Be strong and courageous. Do not be discouraged, for the LORD your God will be with you wherever you go."
Joshua 1:9

REFLECTION QUESTIONS:
+ Has looking down left you too busy planning for your future that you've missed opportunities to grow toward your future? What would it look like today to stop planning and start growing?

CAMERON

EASTERN KENTUCKY UNIVERSITY
OCCUPATIONAL SCIENCE
JUNIOR

Living Extraordinary

GLORIFYING GOD IN THE ORDINARY

"You must make a decision." These were the words spoken into my ear during college orientation. As I sat in a room full of computers and fellow upcoming freshman, I froze. For months, my thoughts—and more importantly, my prayers—had been leading to this moment. This was a decision I had prepared myself for. Why was I in such a panic? Multiple lists of pros and cons had been written out. I had received wise counsel from mentors around me. I spent hours intently seeking the Holy Spirit's leading. Why was I unable to choose?

Maybe I forgot the protection of God.
Maybe I misplaced my true identity.
Maybe I idolized my education.

I think back to my shaking self and I see the truth: I had put pressure on myself to create the extraordinary life I desired. A life full of making disciples and seeing God move in ways only He can. However, I didn't see how an "ordinary major" at an "ordinary college" would make this happen. In this moment I wondered if God had made a mistake bringing me where I was. I wanted to live the life I knew He had promised me in Scripture. I just didn't trust He was fulfilling it.

"I have come that they may have life, and have it to the full."
John 10:10

Ministry is a word rooted within the Christian community, and there are many different ways that ministry can be expressed and carried out. It can take place through conferences or catchy slogans or even cute merchandise. It can be specifically tailored for men or women and the specific struggles each gender has. Ministries come in all forms and sizes but hopefully all forms have the same goal: to teach the Gospel and make disciples. The first Christian ministry conference I experienced was called Women of Faith. While I was still a little girl at the time and didn't fully grasp what I was seeing, I followed my mom into a massive arena filled with women worshipping God and sensed something extraordinary.

Something different.
Something unexplainable.
Something meaningful.

I remember this in such detail. The essence of the arena was alive and holy—as if even the walls were proclaiming praise to God. I remember phrases spoken from the stage, the music playing in the background, and even the color of the t-shirts. For years to come, I would have no clue what this moment meant to my relationship with Jesus, or how it would guide me to the Cross continually. I only knew the experience, but I wouldn't receive the revelation until later.

"Consider it pure joy, my brothers and sisters, whenever you face trials of many kinds, because you know that the testing of your faith produces perseverance."
James 1:2-3

My high school years were ripe with trials. My parents' divorce, depression, partying; the whole shebang. I was angry at one parent and I was bitterly caring for the other. Anxiety ruled over me and I desperately desired affirmation from the world around me. I was living far from extraordinary, I was in no position to serve and lead those around me, and I was far from seeing abundant life. When my faith was tested, I chose hate, anger, and bitterness. The relationships around me were hanging by a thread, especially my relationship with Christ. The enemy used every opportunity to steal my patience and stunt my spiritual growth, which blurred my view of belonging to my Father—of being extraordinary.

Then, one day, I noticed the sin around me. The more I took my eyes off of Jesus, the more I saw the regret and consequences of my sin. During those days, if I wasn't looking toward Jesus, I was intently watching the world. My friendships were failing, I was searching for fulfillment in a guy, and ultimately I began believing the lies of the enemy. I refused the Word because I was angry with the life I had been given. I refused prayer because I was convinced God wasn't listening to me anyway. My soul was thirsty for extraordinary, but I fed it with the ordinary. And yet somehow, shining through the guilt and shame, was grace. It stretched the length of the cross to reach me where I was. I took hold of it and re-learned how to do life with Jesus. My desire to be bold, fearless, and extraordinary was revived.

"'For my thoughts are not your thoughts, neither are your ways my ways,'
declares the LORD."
Isaiah 55:8

I had an image of what extraordinary life in Christ looked like and continued to see the details of ministry around me. However, the quality of my intentions was slightly off. I still wanted to make disciples, but I wanted the recognition. If I led a Bible study, then my mentor would be proud of me. If I began a blog, then people would applaud me. I would do it all on my own, and Jesus would swoop in when I needed help. This mindset reeked of me, myself, and I. In my vision, if an extraordinary life was going to begin, I was going to be the one to make it happen.

This selfish worldview ignited my struggle in the room full of computers and anxious freshmen. Through all my so-called strength and ability, I didn't feel bold or fearless. I was unsatisfied and discontent in where I had been placed. Selecting a major wasn't difficult because of uncertainty in a decision, but because of an insecurity in myself. I feared I would not have the abundance I knew God had promised, and grieved the idea of not living in ministry. I worried that in a small town at a "mediocre" university, I would never achieve God's big dream for my life. Would having an ordinary career spread the extraordinary Gospel?

This continuing anxiety led to an unconscious disobedience to Christ. Without realizing it, I doubted His authority, wisdom, and character. I shut down the memory of my younger self in that arena. I complained during prayer because I wanted a platform to influence women rather than the normal college experience. I lost sight of the Holy Spirit's power.

How would I have ministry here?
How could I serve women here?
How could I accomplish my goals here?

"I am the vine; you are the branches. If you remain in me and I in you,
you will bear much fruit; apart from me you can do nothing."
John 15:5

I knew my focus needed to shift. I searched the Word, dove into prayer, and fully submitted to God's instruction. And by this, I was changed. I discovered that if we choose to allow Satan to captivate our thoughts, if we give into complaining and questioning based upon doubt, if we lose sight of or disregard what the Holy Spirit does, or if we stay removed from the true vine—we are endangered, crippled, dormant, detached, and paused in our purpose.

Drag arrow.
Select.
Submit.

"Congratulations, your major has been declared!"

For most of my story, my spiritual vision had been impaired. Ultimately, I saw my major as a giant step to a greater purpose instead of a small step in a purpose-full reality. In my mind this one choice would determine my experiences, relationships, and opportunities.

It would determine if I was extraordinary.

But that's not what God's Word says. A relationship with Jesus and desperate dependence on Him—empowered by the Holy Spirit—is that only thing that unlocks our extraordinary potential. Remaining in Him by allowing Him to instruct and teach us will take us to our unique designated purpose. Here's the truth: a college major neither defines nor aligns your future. It may suggest it, but it has not determined it. Only God has done that.

Majors may change. Majors may fail. Majors will fade.

"Whoever wants to be my disciple must deny themselves and take up
their cross daily and follow me."
Luke 9:23

Staying near to the presence of God will keep us declared as righteous forever. I clicked the submit button nearly three years ago. The Holy Spirit used Luke 9:23 to whisper a conclusion to my heart: ministry is not limited to conferences, catchy slang, or cute merchandise; ministry is our daily routine. My paranoia was cured by this one word. I realized I was so focused on the "big" I wanted to achieve for God that I totally missed the "little" I could be doing for God. I was fixed on the arena's applause rather than simply taking a seat.

"The eye is the lamp of the body. If your eyes are healthy, your whole body will be full of light."
Matthew 6:22

Class at 10:15 am.
Gym at 6:00 pm.
Study group at 9:00 pm.

After allowing the Holy Spirit to clear my vision, I began to see these normal to-do's as opportunities to show the light of Jesus. I started noticing the chance for God's extraordinary to happen in my ordinary. As I saw this, I prayed the Holy Spirit would specifically give me an outreach, a sphere of influence where I could show Christ's love on a deeper level.

He unveiled what had been right in front of me. Women dominate the gender ratio in the occupational therapy major, which means throughout my weekly classes, I'm surrounded by women. Some are believers in Christ and some are not quite there yet. The Holy Spirit guided a friend and me to lead nearly twenty of these women through the Bible each week. With His power, we're encouraging each other through the struggles of life. Together, we're walking to the cross hand-in-hand.

"I will instruct you and teach you in the way you should go; I will counsel you with my loving eye on you."
Psalms 32:8

I continued to ask the Holy Spirit to help me see through His eyes. With His divine help, I noticed those who needed encouragement. I sat by the girls who I sensed were questioning Jesus. I saw how my subtle actions of obedience to Christ began meaningful conversations. I was bearing fruit.

My soul began to flourish in my normal, mundane, ordinary routine. God had supplied the extraordinary and the abundant life through Jesus. Even though He had been by my side the whole time, I finally noticed Him. His loving eye had been on me even as a young girl in that large arena, and I finally recognized it. Remembering that moment fuels my desire to see God's extraordinary provision in the ordinary. I pray the Holy Spirit points me to the girl needing encouragement. I pray I never underestimate the power of one conversation, one random smile, or one random hello. I can see now where those small aspects of the everyday make a difference. Ultimately, I pray we have daily encounters with our

Creator. I pray our vision continues to clear, allowing the Holy Spirit to instruct, teach, and counsel us to joyfully complete our daily ministries.

"For we are God's handiwork, created in Christ Jesus to do good works, which God prepared in advance for us to do."
Ephesians 2:10

My ordinary life has become extraordinary, by living to glorify an extraordinary God.

KEY VERSES:
John 10:10
James 1:2-3
Isaiah 55:8
John 15:5
Luke 9:23
Matthew 6:22
Psalms 32:8
Ephesians 2:10

DISCUSSION QUESTIONS:

+ What pressures are you putting on yourself to create the extraordinary life you desire? What is your definition of extraordinary and where does it stem from?

+ How has Christian culture influenced your walk with the Lord? Are you following His voice or pursuing things that seem impressive to the people around you? How does an extraordinary life in the eyes of Christ differ from an extraordinary life in the eyes of the world?

+ Have you let choices like deciding on a major define your future? Instead of putting so much weight on these decisions, how can you begin to view them as small steps of obedience toward a greater purpose?

+ Often when our circumstances seem ordinary and mundane, we subconsciously detach ourselves from Him and begin doubting His power. Have you let your circumstances separate you from God? How might God be building your ordinary into something extraordinary?

+ Cameron shares, "After allowing the Holy Spirit to clear my vision, I began to see these normal to-do's as opportunities to show the light of Jesus." How can you begin to see more purpose in your day-to-day? How could your ordinary life become extraordinary if you lived each day to glorify an extraordinary God?

DEVOTIONALS

CONTRIBUTOR: *Anna Leigh Mayfield*

DAY 1

When we trust God to direct us, we can finally let go of the pressure we put on ourselves. But, even when we trust His direction, we can fall prey to the lie that an extraordinary life has to look a certain way. Like Cameron, we might believe that because we live a "normal" life, we aren't really living to the capacity God has in mind.

This can be discouraging, especially if we begin to compare our lives with those of people who do more noticeable things. Praise Jesus that extraordinary is not confined to a specific appearance. Christ came so that all might live in abundance. He thinks that you are extraordinary, and His plans for you are nothing less than amazing. Your life may not look exactly like that of a famous missionary or preacher, but if your life is being directed by God, it's guaranteed to be extraordinary.

How have you defined extraordinary? And has that led you to compare yourself to others or doubt your purpose? Your life is extraordinary, not because of the things you do, but because of the God you serve. Meditate on that beautiful truth! He makes our lives an incredible outpouring of His power, and all we have to do is trust Him to make it so.

KEY VERSES:
"I am the vine; you are the branches. If you remain in me and I in you, you will bear much fruit; apart from me you can do nothing."
John 15:5

REFLECTION QUESTIONS:
+ What pressures are you putting on yourself to create the extraordinary life you desire? What is your definition of extraordinary and where does it stem from?

+ How has Christian culture influenced your walk with the Lord? Are you following His voice or pursuing things that seem impressive to the people around you? How does an extraordinary life in the eyes of Christ differ from an extraordinary life in the eyes of the world?

DAY 2

Life is full of decisions. Some are easier, like what topping to get on your pizza, but some are quite literally life-changing. Maybe you feel the pressure to pick the perfect major, boyfriend, or internship. Sometimes we become too focused on these big decisions and we lose sight of God's promises.

Do you ever put pressure on yourself to create an extraordinary life through these decisions? Are you placing the sole responsibility of the outcome of your life on yourself? Think of areas in your life where you may second guess yourself because you're trying to uphold this unrealistic standard of perfection.

It comes down to trust. Do you trust that God is going to work in and through you? Do you believe that He wants to work in you? Instead of turning to comparison and the voices around us to guide our decisions, let's trust that God has something extraordinary in store for us—in His timing. The next time that you're tempted to turn to your own strength when you don't fully trust that God is going to work in you, stop and let the Lord remind you of His promises. He is willing and able to work mightily through us. All we must do is trust Him. He has a greater extraordinary purpose in mind.

KEY VERSES:
"Trust in the LORD with all your heart and lean not on your own understanding; in all your ways submit to him, and he will make your paths straight."
Proverbs 3:5-6

REFLECTION QUESTIONS:
+ Have you let choices like deciding on a major define your future? Instead of putting so much weight on these decisions, how can you begin to view them as small steps of obedience toward a greater purpose?

Sometimes our plans fail. It's an inevitable fact of life that can bring a lot of discouragement. When our plans fall through or we mess up, it's easy to fall into the belief that nothing good will come out of it. We detach ourselves from the Lord and believe the lie that we are failures and He can't use our lives for anything fruitful and good. However, like we've already discovered in Cameron's story, our God is extraordinary. He has the power to take our failures and turn them around. Yes, life will have its ups and downs, and yes, we will falter. But our sweet Jesus never leaves our side. He picks us up, dusts us off, and gives us the tools we need to keep going.

When we fail, He does not—and He never will. This is a promise that we can hold onto tightly throughout our trials and triumphs. On those days when you feel like you can't possibly do anything right, hold to the promise that your faithful and powerful God is still with you and is still working. No matter what, He can make your story beautiful.

What part of your life discourages you the most? Is it regret from your past or fear about your future? What would happen if you began to claim God's faithfulness over those areas? The enemy can do his best, but he will never be able to stop God from working. This means that you can't even stop God. And if you can't stop Him, neither can your mistakes. So take heart, friend. Jesus has conquered the world, and He will empower your life for His glory. There's nothing you can do to discourage Him. When we feel low, He will lift us up, no matter where we are.

KEY VERSES:
"But those who hope in the Lord will renew their strength. They will soar on wings like eagles; they will run and not grow weary, they will walk and not be faint."
Isaiah 40:31

"I have told you these things, so that in me you may have peace. In this world you will have trouble. But take heart! I have overcome the world."
John 16:33

"And we know that in all things God works for the good of those who love Him, who have been called according to his purpose."
Romans 8:28

REFLECTION QUESTIONS:

+ Often when our circumstances seem ordinary and mundane, we subconsciously detach ourselves from Him and begin doubting His power. Have you let your circumstances separate you from God? How might God be building your ordinary into something extraordinary?

DAY 4

Our lives are extraordinary because our God is extraordinary. So what does this mean for our actions, choices, and words? What does extraordinary living look like? Like Cameron, we need to start asking God to take over our daily routines. Who do you see every day that He might want you to start talking to? When was the last time you asked your lab partner how she was doing? Is there someone at the coffee shop you frequent who might appreciate a study buddy? These seemingly mundane interactions can be used by God to open doors to deeper conversations, or to let people see for the first time that Jesus cares about them.

Think over your daily routine. Do you approach your day with the mindset of letting God work through the ordinary? He is all-present and all-powerful, which means no matter where we are or what we are doing, no matter how big or how small a situation seems, He is able to move. And, since He is within us, He is able to work through us. We have been given full ability to start those conversations, smile at those other people, and give those compliments, even if it's outside of our comfort zones. Our extraordinary God empowers us to make waves within the ordinary.

KEY VERSES:
"Now to him who is able to do immeasurably more than all we ask or imagine, according to his power that is at work within us, to him be glory in the church and in Christ Jesus throughout all generations, for ever and ever! Amen."
Ephesians 3:20-21

"I can do all this through him who gives me strength."
Philippians 4:13

"So whether you eat or drink or whatever you do, do it all for the glory of God."
1 Corinthians 10:31

REFLECTION QUESTIONS:
+ Cameron shares, "After allowing the Holy Spirit to clear my vision, I began to see these normal to-do's as opportunities to show the light of Jesus." How can you begin to see more purpose in your day-to-day? How could your ordinary life become extraordinary if you lived each day to glorify an extraordinary God?

HANNAH

UNIVERSITY OF MONTANA
EXERCISE SCIENCE
SENIOR

Striving To Be Perfect

A BEAUTY YOU CANNOT CREATE FOR YOURSELF

Alarm clock rings at 5:00 a.m. *Resist the urge to hit snooze.*
Work out until 8:00 a.m. *Maybe I can eat a banana if I have the time.*
Going straight into 9:00 a.m. classes until noon. *Gosh, I hate physics.*
Rushing over to volunteer at the physical therapy clinic until 3:00 p.m.
Hopefully this will help me get into grad school. . .
Working at the University until 6:00 p.m. *Maybe I'll eat a salad for a
quick lunch/dinner.*
Study session until 8:00 p.m. *I still don't like physics.*
Head back to the dorms to be with my residents. *I love being a Resident
Assistant.*
Finally, bed by 10:00 p.m. *If I'm lucky.*

This was my daily schedule. I was consumed by my thoughts, while
my body was in constant motion. Describing my physical, mental,
emotional status during this time as exhausted, chaotic, and beaten-
down would be an understatement.

*"And to know this love that surpasses knowledge—that you may be
filled to the measure of all the fullness of God."*
Ephesians 3:19

Filled with the fullness of God? Now that sounds truly heavenly. And
not just filled, but filled to the measure. To be completely and utterly
filled with the Lord, no room for anything else. To be bursting with
God's love, His mercy, His faithfulness—I cannot even begin to imagine
anything better. But during my junior year of college, I was full of just
about everything but God.

Before that year, I was a girl filled with the Lord and felt like I was
bearing many fruits of the Spirit. I thought of myself as a joyful
daughter who showed kindness toward others, was gentle in her ways,
and ultimately was a faithful follower. And I thus entered college eager

to learn, eager to love, and eager to grow. But after the first few years, those traits were put on the backburner. After a difficult divorce between my parents, the stresses of college I placed upon myself, and becoming consumed by the competitiveness of graduate school acceptance, I could barely recognize myself.

I struggled with restlessness, annoyance, and vanity. I was constantly striving to earn love, affection, accomplishment, and boost my sense of pride. I was trying to earn back the identity and worth that I had lost somewhere along the way. Completely unaware that this identity could only be found through the Father, I yearned to control anything and everything I could. I was trying to play the role of God.

This was not an overnight transformation. The old me, the one resting in Christ, slowly dwindled away. It started with me believing that my behaviors and actions wouldn't become a habit. Little did I know these consistent changes would manifest into an eating disorder. The journey I took from a full, alive spirit to this place of emptiness was not a pretty one.

At first I thought counting calories would be good for my health and that exercising every day for two or three hours would only make me stronger. However, that soon turned into obsessing over every aspect of my food intake. I was planning out meals weeks in advance and stressing over receiving the proper amount of carbohydrates, fats, and protein—or what I thought to be proper, which was realistically much too small to be remotely close to adequate. I began running over fifty miles a week without the proper nutrition to do so, pushing my body farther and faster when it was pleading for rest.

But it wasn't just my eating and activity habits. I was constantly working to better my résumé, thinking it was there that I could reclaim my worth and identity. Balancing four jobs, perfect grades, and volunteering meant I was always on the go, and so were my thoughts. My mind was always wandering from its current surroundings to the next thing on my agenda. During conversations with others I found myself absent-minded and thinking about the next task that I needed to accomplish. I couldn't seem to stay focused on the present with all its blessings or the wonderful people around me. And I definitely wasn't focused on Christ.

"But seek first his kingdom and his righteousness, and all these things will be given to you as well."
Matthew 6:33

I thought all these achievements would be impressive, that once I was a certain weight or got into a certain graduate school I would be joyful again. I thought these actions would bring me the satisfaction, pride, and identity I was searching for. But unsurprisingly, it wasn't enough. All these things still weren't enough. There was nothing I could ever earn or achieve that would put my soul to rest. The void I was seeking to fill was God-sized. I honestly thought that striving and earning was what I had to do. I thought that lifestyle was expected of me. My thoughts had become so distorted—I convinced myself this suffering was what God wanted for me. Boy, was I wrong.

Before I knew it, I was so weak I couldn't walk, constantly in and out of the hospital getting treatment for the consequences of my lack of nutrition. I became a slave to the world I created. I lost everything: my gentleness, my goodness, my faithfulness, my joy. And not just my joy for life, but my joy for the Lord. I effectively buried the gifts of the Spirit when I created a world in which I was omnipotent and omniscient. It was a world without peace, love, and stillness. It was a world without Christ.

I forgot that our Father wanted me to be full of Him, His love, and His promises. I knew I had hit rock bottom, the lowest of lows. I didn't know how I got there nor how to get out of it. I had tried so many times to start the healing process. I'd have a couple good days, but always spiraled right back to where I had begun, feeling so defeated and completely and utterly alone. That June, I was completely out of ideas and at my lowest ever recorded weight. But then, I slowly began to fill back up again, because God reminded me that I wasn't alone—that I never had been and never would be. That was the day I began to heal, because I finally realized I could not heal without Christ.

I remember deciding that I no longer wanted to live this meager, exhausting life. I wanted it to be abundant again, so I refused to keep residing in the empty world I created. I no longer indulged in being a woman of the flesh, but instead relearned how to be a woman of the Lord. I didn't want to be a slave to my sins any longer, crippled by my need to perform, to succeed, and to earn.

"For we know that our old self was crucified with him so that the body ruled by sin might be done away with, that we should no longer be slaves to sin."
Romans 6:6

My healing process seemed quick. The physical healing was easier than the emotional healing. Luckily, I was able to gain weight quickly with only minor health complications along the way. Healing emotionally, however, is the most intense challenge I had ever faced—and am still facing.

I had to give up this self-inflicted pressure to be perfect and the idea that I needed to suffer through this life. At first, giving back this control to God was really painful. It was as if I were clinging on to these ideas of perfection and someone had to lovingly pry my fingers away one by one. But then I began allowing myself to be loved and to love the individuals around me. Day by day I began to rest in the Word of the Lord and in His promises. God had already given me all the beauty I could ever desire, the type of beauty I could never create for myself. The kind of beauty that is contagious, flows from within, and then radiates out for all to see. This beauty comes from knowing that you are a daughter of the King.

During many days of my recovery, I was consumed by voices declaring I wasn't good enough for healing or happiness, persuading me that I wasn't worthy of rest or peace, convincing me I didn't deserve the love surrounding me, whispering that I would never be fully known nor fully loved by Christ. And to be honest, there are days when those voices still feel like truth. But I've learned healing is not linear. It is not a one-and-done kind of thing. We are human. We sin. We drift from the Lord by focusing on the flesh. Ultimately, we get distracted on our journey to Christ.

The difference is that now I am able to identify these voices as the enemy. He knows my vices and my weakness. In these moments, I must remember God's promises. I must remember that Jesus has never left my side and that I am not healing by my own strength, but through the strength of the Father and His Holy Spirit within me. I fixed my eyes on the Lord and allowed His voice to become the only thing I heard.

Through my recovery this became my prayer and cry to the Lord: I will find my joy through You again, Lord. I will create joy in the storms, during the hardships, and through the unknown by fixing my eyes on You and listening to Your voice. I will put my faith in You. I cannot do this without You Lord. You know all, You are in control and You have the power. My worth rests in my identity as a daughter of the King. And it is an identity I could never earn and can never be taken away.

"The thief comes only to steal and kill and destroy; I have come that they may have life, and have it to the full."
John 10:10

Meditating on this verse led to major breakthrough in my healing. I realized I was created for so much more than the life I was living. I was striving, while God declared I am already more than enough. I was weary, while the Lord just wanted me to rest in Him. I was full of shame, while the power of Christ was made perfect in my weakness. I was burdened, while the Lord wanted me to be free from the weight of this world. There was a huge disconnect between the life I was living and the life the Lord desired for me. I was living according to my will, which had emptied me of Him. But there was something so much greater promised to me by my Father. All I needed to do was chase after it. We love a Lord who is full of joy, peace, and goodness. And He craves these things for His children. Through the Holy Spirit dwelling within us we can also be full of joy, peace, and goodness. And while the valleys will come, they will also go. The Lord created us to be full of Him. Jesus conquered the greatest darkness in order that we may bask in His glorious and pure light.

Ever since I have focused on these truths, my life has become full again, beyond my wildest imagination. Here is an excerpt from a journal I kept through my recovery: I am absolutely flabbergasted by the blessings and beauty in my life. I find so much joy in every single day. I have never felt more connected and loved by the Lord, my friends, my family, and myself. I now know this is how life is intended to be lived—full of bliss and radiance and lots and lots of giggles.

But, as heartbreaking as it is to admit this, I still struggle. I know this is going to be the battle I have to face daily, but now I will face it with the Lord. I will run to Him instead of running away from Him. I know my worth. I know my identity in Christ as His daughter who was fearfully and wonderfully made. And I know the great plans God has set before me.

There is no doubt that God was with me throughout this entire journey, molding each of my experiences with His hand. I truly believe He was exposing the wounds that I had hidden for so long. Wounds I was afraid to open, afraid to look at, afraid to admit were really there. Wounds that were messy and deep and ugly. Wounds that were desperate for healing. Wounds caused by my own self-control, perfectionism, and insecurity. Wounds caused by sexual sin, jealousy, and lying. Wounds caused by others' sin: sexual assault, unhealthy relationships, and neglectful parents. And the list goes on and on.

But hallelujah! Our God is a good, good Father and no wound is too messy for Him. No sin is too much for Him. He will never turn His back on us. We are His children, and He is always waiting for us to come running back into His arms. He exposes our wounds solely to restore, never to shame. He cleanses these wounds so we may continue to better reflect His perfect love to this world. And this is exactly what I am doing now, uncovering each wound so my Father can make them better.

I encourage you to follow me in this pursuit, to go to the Father with every wound and every hurt. Only through Jesus can we be healed, winning the battle against the flesh and experiencing the victory of joy, goodness, and self-control. Only through Jesus can we be filled with the fullness of the Lord.

Nowadays, my schedule looks more like this:

Alarm clock rings at 7:00 a.m. *Still resisting the urge to hit snooze.* Starting my day with a daily devotional and a thankful prayer. *Thank You, Lord.* Working out until 8:00 a.m. *Health means more than just self-control.* Going to class from 10:00 a.m. until 1:00 p.m. *Gosh, I love exercise physiology.* Rushing over to meet with my friends for lunch together. *Wow, my face hurts from laughing.* Working at the University until 6:00 p.m. and then having a relaxed dinner with friends. *Or maybe while watching Netflix. . .* Lounging around before bedtime. *What a day.*

I am now consumed by grace, and love, and laughter—and my newfound demeanor reflects that. My physical, mental, and emotional status now reflects the contentment and peace God has graciously given me. And I am so thankful for every single moment.

KEY VERSES:
Ephesians 3:19
Matthew 6:33
Romans 6:6
John 10:10

DISCUSSION QUESTIONS:
+ In what area of your life do lies from the enemy hold the most weight? What is the enemy telling you about who you are?

+ When life feels chaotic, what do you try and control? What are you striving to accomplish in moments of uncertainty?

+ One obvious indicator of God's presence in your life is fruit of the Spirit. Has your striving led you away from God's Spirit? What fruits of the Spirit have you neglected and how could you better develop them in your life?

+ What shame have you been carrying alone? How has this isolation led you to believe lies about yourself? Could vulnerability about this shame help you to overcome it?

+ Hannah shares, "God had already given me all the beauty I could ever desire, the type of beauty I could never create for myself." Have you accepted the truth that God created you the way you are for a purpose? How would the way you view yourself and others change if you stepped further into this truth?

DEVOTIONALS

CONTRIBUTOR: *Bailey Hurley*

DAY 1

In Hannah's story, we learn that our identities can be shaped by a myriad of harmless decisions to put our trust in other "gods" more than our great God. For Hannah, planning her days, staying organized for the future, and trying her best at everything she did seemed like living an accomplished life. Many outsiders would assume she had it all together, but these good habits were actually false gods making Hannah believe she had to do more, be better, and never mess up.

Don't we all do this in some way? We unknowingly become slaves to lies that eventually consume us. Maybe you feel like you have to be successful in everything you do, so you become a slave to your schoolwork and extracurricular activities. Maybe you feel like you have to be loved by everyone, so you become a slave to people-pleasing, not taking care of yourself. Or maybe you are like Hannah, feeling like you have to be perfect, so you become a slave to an impossible standard you will never meet.

Yet through Jesus, we receive victory over all the lies, labels, and false gods that have led us astray from God. We no longer have to be slaves to those destructive masters because we serve a God who delights in us just as we are—imperfections and all.

KEY VERSES:
"For we know that our old self was crucified with him so that the body ruled by sin might be done away with, that we should no longer be slaves to sin."
Romans 6:6

"So you are no longer a slave, but God's child; and since you are his child, God has made you also an heir."
Galatians 4:7

REFLECTION QUESTIONS:

+ In what area of your life do lies from the enemy hold the most weight? What is the enemy telling you about who you are?

+ When life feels chaotic, what do you try and control? What are you striving to accomplish in moments of uncertainty?

DAY 2

Hannah's story illustrates for us that striving pulls us away from the fruits of the Spirit and instead burdens us with anxiety and stress. Even good intentions can become tainted when we feel like we have to prove our worth to the world or to God. Endlessly chasing after happiness, success, and a good life will ultimately leave behind the grace and freedom we have in Jesus. Striving under the law crushes each of us. We seek after things which, even though they appear good, lead us into a life of sin, instead of seeking God and living a life of righteousness.

Have you ever noticed how tired you are? Have you felt impatient at the littlest thing? Is there a fruit of the Spirit that has been neglected because of your endless striving?

The good news is that we can turn to God, humbly lay down our striving tendencies, and embrace our worth that is found in Him alone. When we walk closely with God, He cultivates the fruits of the Spirit daily. Not because of anything we have done or earned, but because He desires for us to see the goodness of resting in His presence.

KEY VERSES:
"But the fruit of the Spirit is love, joy, peace, patience, kindness, goodness, faithfulness, gentleness and self-control. Against such things there is no law."
Galatians 5:22-23

"But seek first his kingdom and his righteousness, and all these things will be given to you as well."
Matthew 6:33

REFLECTION QUESTIONS:
+ One obvious indicator of God's presence in your life is fruit of the Spirit. Has your striving led you away from God's Spirit? What fruits of the Spirit have you neglected and how could you better develop them in your life?

One of the greatest strategies the enemy uses against us is making us feel isolated in our messy, dark places. It's a weapon that makes us wonder, how would anyone ever look at me the same way again if they knew what was really going on? The enemy wants us to believe that we are unworthy of love, acceptance, and healing, so that we will push further and further away from a loving Christian community.

Have you hidden under a guise of perfection so that people don't see the real you? Like Hannah, we can and should choose to be vulnerable and open up to other believers about the trials we are facing. The kindness and mercy of others is one of the ways God shows His love for us. Our community will hold us up in prayer, remind us of God's truth, and remind our hearts that we are beautiful daughters of God made whole by Him.

No longer is our identity rooted in slavery to sin or in proving our worth—it's anchored in God's great love for us. He comes to bring life and life to the full, and God uses His people to usher that truth into our dark places.

KEY VERSES:
"The thief comes only to steal and kill and destroy; I have come that they may have life, and have it to the full."
John 10:10

"Above all, love each other deeply, because love covers over a multitude of sins."
1 Peter 4:8

REFLECTION QUESTIONS:
+ What shame have you been carrying alone? How has this isolation led you to believe lies about yourself? Could vulnerability about this shame help you to overcome it?

DAY 4

How do you begin your days? What are the first thoughts on your mind? Is it the long to-do list? Is it the weight of how you will perform today in school? Is it the fear of whether your friends are going to accept you today for who you are, rather than what you do for them?

We begin our days with a flood of thoughts that impact how we will live confidently as daughters of God. Instead of allowing the fears, lies, or stressors to decide who we will be, let's allow God to dictate our character and actions each day.

God has made you for this day. He calls you daughter and sends you out to be an expression of His love. You have been filled to the measure of all the fullness of God. You don't have to be perfect, or the best or the most liked, you just have to trust God to shine through you in every moment. The more that you place your identity in His truth, the more room you will have to accept and love other people just as they are.

Pray today that you would be a woman who delights in the way God has made her and confidently passes that joy on to others.

KEY VERSES:
"But you are a chosen people, a royal priesthood, a holy nation, God's special possession, that you may declare the praises of him who called you out of darkness into his wonderful light."
1 Peter 2:9

"And to know this love that surpasses knowledge—that you may be filled to the measure of all the fullness of God."
Ephesians 3:19

REFLECTION QUESTIONS:
+ Hannah shares, "God had already given me all the beauty I could ever desire, the type of beauty I could never create for myself." Have you accepted the truth that God created you the way you are for a purpose? How would the way you view yourself and others change if you stepped further into this truth?

LAUREN

BELMONT UNIVERSITY
PUBLISHING
FRESHMAN

Trusting God's Vision

BRINGING YOUR DREAMS BACK TO GOD

The first class I took for my major was a big moment. It was one of those life moments—a hallowed peephole glimpse into the rest of my life— and it made my heart beat a little faster and left me slightly breathless. Okay, maybe I was just a little winded and lightheaded because I had to take the stairs to my fifth-floor class, but still. It was my first semester of college, and I knew this was it. There would be no change of major for me. For years I had dreamed of taking publishing classes, ultimately serving the Lord as an editor with a corner office and a large desk strewn with manuscripts waiting for my stamp of approval.

This was no new dream. I had prayed every night my freshman year of high school that God would bring me to the perfect college and the perfect program, and since Belmont offered the only undergraduate publishing degree in the nation, this must have been divinely ordained. My prayers had been answered in a big way, and I felt invincible. Why wouldn't I work hard? Harder than everyone else? Piece by piece, my life was officially coming together. God had given this to me, and I was going to make the most of it.

So I chased the dream. I told myself that's what college was all about, after all. I ran after my desire for success, not minding that I was pushing myself further and further away from those around me and from the heart of God. Having someone ask to eat breakfast with me became irritating, because it meant having to put off my work until later. I ate most meals alone, waving off invitations to join my friends, because I had "too much to do." It was nice having company in the library, but I felt more productive alone, so I would sneak out of the dorm to avoid having someone join me. When I heard laughter outside my closed door at night, I would plug my headphones into my computer and keep typing.

Every so often, I would feel the choking effect of too much stress. Convinced I was just overreacting, I beat down any internal questioning over whether this was the way things should be. If I was stressed, that just meant I needed to work a little harder so I could have a little more time to relax. As the stress rashes crawled up my arms, I tugged my sleeves down to hide them. Out of sight, out of mind. Starry-eyed and confident, I sat in the front row of my publishing class every Tuesday and Thursday. I went into our first group project practically bubbling over with excitement, putting my name down as the editor-in-chief. And the fact that the head of our program and a real-life industry professional would be judging our project presentation? Even better. Corner office, here I come! My heart leapt. . .

. . .and painfully discovered gravity. "Disaster" is the descriptor that comes to mind in hindsight, but I suppose "trainwreck" or "catastrophe" would also be appropriate. Our presentation was in the wrong format. We had too much information about things that did not matter and too little on things that did. I stumbled through my part, my words not coming out even half as articulate and professional as I had imagined they would. From where I stood I could see the judges' scoring sheets. They circled a 1 out of 5. Then a 2 out of 5. Creativity: 2. Feasibility: 1. My heart deflated and fell crumpled into the pit of my stomach. The presentation was completely out of my control, and there was nothing I could do to save it. Once the nightmare ended, I meekly shuffled up to the industry professional to ask for her business card in a desperate attempt to salvage my dignity.

"Oh," she said, tilting her nose into the air and shooting a glance at the door, "I ran out of them. But here, I guess I can write my email down for you." She tore a tiny corner from her notebook and scribbled her name and email onto it. I thanked her half-heartedly, speed-walked out of the room, and practically fled down the stairs with my eyes on the floor to hide my red-hot face. I stumbled into the open air and started along the lonely sidewalk to the library. The only thing to do was to work harder, of course. I would hunch over my laptop until I was a 5 out of 5. That would fix it. I could fix this. With each step my resolve hardened, and my humiliation soon turned to anger.

First and foremost, I was angry with myself. I chastised myself for every mistake made on the project and for everything I had failed to prepare for in the presentation. How could I have been so stupid? Wasn't I supposed to be good at this? Hadn't God brought me here for a reason?

As that last thought settled itself in my mind, my frustration with myself flared out toward God.

Lord! I cried internally. How could You let this happen? I thought You brought me here. I prayed that You would! I know it was no accident I found this program. How could You bring me to this point and then just let me go? Maybe You didn't think that when I prayed for this, I had wanted to be good at it too. I wasn't just angry, I was terrified. My throat constricted as I walked, my breath came hard and fast. What was I doing here if I wasn't going to be good at this? Had this all been some awful mistake? Had I worked so hard for nothing? I felt so lost and unsure, as though the sidewalk had been torn out from under me, sending me spiraling into a deep hole of doubt. The pieces of my life that were supposed to be coming together began breaking apart, one by one. I doubted myself, my program, my professors, and most of all, God's plan for my life.

But in my panic, the Lord silenced me. He silenced me not with words of anger or frustration as I blindly lashed out in fury and fear, but with words of patience and love. A verse I had heard in a Bible study the week before began inexplicably resonating in my thoughts.

"Look at the birds of the air; they do not sow or reap or store away in barns, and yet your heavenly Father feeds them. Are you not much more valuable than they?"
Matthew 6:26

Are you not much more valuable than they? Are you not much more valuable than they?

Those words in particular were repeated over and over again. It was as though God had put up a hand to calm me, stop me in my tracks, and simply say, "Lauren, there's a whole lot of 'I' in this story. Do you not remember how valuable you are to me? Did you forget how I have provided for you over and over again? Have you forgotten the prayer of faith you used to pray?"

It was true. Four years before this moment, I had prayed for a year straight that God would make me into the woman He wanted me to be to accomplish the plans He had for me—those exact words, every night. God, make me into the woman You want me to be to accomplish the plans You have for me. That faith, that humility, that dependency—where had it gone?

"'There you saw how the LORD your God carried you, as a father carries his son, all the way you went until you reached this place.' In spite of this, you did not trust in the LORD your God, who went ahead of you on your journey, in fire by night and in a cloud by day, to search out places for you to camp and to show you the way you should go."
Deuteronomy 1:31-33

"In his pride the wicked man does not seek him; in all his thoughts there is no room for God."
Psalms 10:4

Determined to do it on my own and prove myself worthy of God's calling, I had pursued my ambition and strayed from the one who had always led me and provided for me. I blindly followed my pride, and it led me straight to brokenness. It led to feeling lost, hurt, lonely, anxious, and afraid. It led to a mind consumed by worry. It led to choosing work over relationships again, and again, and again. At that very moment, I was on a literal path that was taking me to sit in the cold and isolated library, disconnected from the world around me. That would change nothing. I would still be heartbroken and lost, and no matter how many hours I spent studying, I could not put the pieces back together on my own.

Lord, I asked, where do I go from here? I am so lost, and I know I can't do it on my own anymore. Here are my pieces. Here are my academics, my career, and my dreams. Please take them and put me together the way You know is best for me.

Success. That's what I was after. Brick by brick, I built what I thought would be my dream castle, not seeing how I had actually built a wall between myself and the outside world. I poured my heart and soul into it. I poured my time and energy, every last bit I had, into this work. How fragile it was, to have crashed down so easily. Standing in the rubble and broken pieces, the situation looked irreparable.

"Yet you, LORD, are our Father. We are the clay, you are the potter; we are all the work of your hand."
Isaiah 64:8

In the Japanese form of pottery called kintsugi, the artist uses pieces of broken pottery as the material. When first watching the process, an onlooker might not understand what the sculptor has in mind for the broken pieces, laying there shattered and seemingly useless or unfixable.

The thing that sets kintsugi apart from other forms of art is not the pottery itself, however, but in what the sculptor does with it. Kintsugi translates to English as "gold splicing." To make it, the artist takes the broken pottery pieces and seals them back together with gold. An observer may wonder why the sculptor allows a lovely bowl or plate to be broken, yet it is this very process of taking something broken and piecing it back together that makes this particular type of pottery so beautiful and unique. Whether the new piece is made from just a few larger broken pieces or from a ceramic that was absolutely shattered, the sculptor seals it together in a way that is utterly stunning and completely brand-new.

Is God not making me into a better, more beautiful creation than I ever could have made myself? Beginning the process of breaking and piecing back together was not what I'd had in mind for my first semester at college. It's been a painful process, and I (the pottery) have been concerned many times as to what exactly my sculptor is doing. Why did this need to happen? Lord, is there any reason for this brokenness? Those questions have been begged so many times. But what I'm learning is that, just like a kintsugi artist, the Lord will not leave any piece of me broken. Every crack becomes a story, a lesson to be learned, a way for God to make me into a new creation. See this golden scar? That's when I learned I cannot do it on my own, and where the Lord sealed my hurt back together with His wisdom. And this one? This crack was mended by grace—where I learned that no pain is without purpose.

"Many are the plans in a person's heart, but it is the LORD's purpose that prevails."
Proverbs 19:21

I desired to be successful. I was confused—wasn't this the desire God had for me too? But what happened in my moment of total failure gave me a glimpse into God's true desires for me. How could God grant me the desires of my heart if those desires were self-destructive? He desires that I not seclude myself, but flourish in community. He desires that I not internalize my worries and fears, but give them up to Him. He desires that I am filled up with the Holy Spirit, that I rest in the promise that the plans He has for me are good, and that I know and believe He will provide for my every need. He desires that I trust Him to put me together the best way possible. I do not have to be the sculptor, I just have to be willing to be pieced together and molded into a beautiful creation.

I poured my heart into building up my dreams, these castle walls, but God wanted me to pour my heart into Him. He will give me the desires of my heart, but only when I learn that my imperfect desires will never amount to my best possible life. When the desire of my heart mirrors God's desire for my life, only then will it be realized. My desire can no longer be for those manuscripts stacked on that corner-office desk. My desire must be the plan God has for me, whatever it may be, and to trust that His plan is greater than my own. It may still be that corner office, but it may be a whole lot better than a corner office. One thing is for sure: it's going to be more than I could imagine. And the best part? All that God requests is my broken pieces and my trust of Him as the master sculptor. No late nights in the library required.

On my way to the library that day, I stopped in the middle of the sidewalk and finally listened to what God desired for me. Swallowing my pride, I turned around and left the library behind me. Scanning my ID at the door to my dorm, I climbed the stairs up to my hall and stopped in the open doorway of a friend's room. Standing there, I felt the tears finally prick behind my eyes. "I've had a really bad day," I told her. "Can I come in?"

Everyone's story is unique—we all break in different ways. One thing is universal, though: we all have moments that pull back the curtain on our brokenness and expose our flaws. But the defining moment is not in the situation, it's in how we respond to it. It's hard to relinquish artistic control of our lives to God. It's hard to trust that His vision is greater than our own, or that He has the best in mind for us, while we're getting injured by the effort to pick up our own broken pieces. But if we look up, we find that God isn't leaning over us telling us that we've failed. He is in front of us, reaching out, saying, Let Me help you. Let Me mend you. I will heal you. I love you in your brokenness, I love you in your mess. Let Me show you how, with Me, those things can be made beautiful.

"Trust in the LORD with all your heart and lean not on your own understanding; in all your ways submit to him, and he will make your paths straight."
Proverbs 3:5-6

One of the most incredible kintsugi pieces I have ever seen is a shining, bright white anatomical heart with a spiderweb of gold-filled cracks spanning its surface, called "Repaired Heart." To me, it's the best depiction of trusting the Lord with your whole life. There will be moments of pain and brokenness, but the Lord never leaves you that way. God in His great craftsmanship washes the dirt of sin away, mends the cracks with His precious grace and mercy, and makes you into a new creation. Even when you aren't sure where God is taking you in the moment, He has an artistic vision, and it is beautiful.

Did the stress and worry immediately evaporate when I placed my pieces in God's hands and once again trusted Him with my life? No, not completely. I still experience uncertainty. There are no verses in the Bible that say everything will be exactly the way you want when you decide to trust the Lord. But there are verses that assure us God has only the best intentions for us, and that His plans and desires for us are good. I am in the restoration process. I am choosing to move forward, following those plans, and the Lord's desires have begun to overtake my heart. I now desire to spend time in Christ-centered community, being filled with the Lord's peace, instead of slaving over work on my own. I desire to serve God in whatever I do, instead of serving my own pride and ambitions. The Lord has honored that, and He is now using me in ways I could not have imagined, ways that are truly greater than my own. Piece by piece, I'm receiving vision of God's desire for my life.

You are not forgotten. The Lord has a plan and purpose for your life. You are valuable, and your brokenness can be transformed. You need only to trust the master sculptor.

"I desire to do your will, my God; your law is within my heart."
Psalm 40:8

KEY VERSES:
Matthew 6:26
Deuteronomy 1:31-33
Psalms 10:4
Isaiah 64:8
Proverbs 19:21
Proverbs 3:5-6
Psalms 40:8

DISCUSSION QUESTIONS:
+ Where have you been looking for value in your life? Is your value placed in what you've accomplished or the things at which you hope to be successful?

+ Have you lacked trust in God's vision for your life? If so, what makes you feel like your plans are better in your own hands than in His?

+ Lauren shares, "I ran after my desire for success, not minding that I was pushing myself further and further away from those around me and from the heart of God." Has chasing after a goal or a dream isolated you from community and the heart of God? What are you sacrificing for the sake of success?

+ When you are truly chasing God's heart, your desires for your life will align with His desires for you. What parts of your dreams have been rooted in selfishness or are distant from your relationship with Him? How could God reshape your dreams when you bring them back to Him?

+ Do you need to fixate more on God's everyday gifts for you rather than your ultimate dream? How might these small moments bring you closer to God's bigger destiny?

DEVOTIONALS

CONTRIBUTOR: *Emma Schrepel*

DAY 1

It often feels as though we are not allowed to make mistakes in college, or sometimes, life in general. Especially as Christians we feel the burden of some made-up standard that tells us to be perfect and never mess up. In Lauren's story, even her constant striving for perfection in her classes and countless hours spent in the library don't prevent her from messing up in her group presentation. Mistakes happen no matter how much we try to stop them, because we're human and it's only natural. The issue arises when we put so much pressure on ourselves to be perfect that those mess-ups become fatal pity parties and self-doubt parades.

What if God's plan for your life at the moment is for you to mess up? What if His plan is the opposite of perfection? What if, at the exact moment we have made the most mistakes, He is the most proud of us? When we mess up, we are arguably at our most humble state, open to learning about who we are in God's eyes. When a child knocks down the tower they built out of blocks, their parents celebrate and help them build it again. What if we celebrated our mistakes in the same way? What if we allowed God to help us build up our life again? Lauren explains this concept when she talks about the art of kintsugi. Do you ever look for value in the mistakes you've made or only the successes?

When we are so adamant about attaining perfection for our lives, we find ourselves not needing to trust God's vision for our lives. If we have everything perfectly handled and planned out, we don't need to trust anybody but ourselves. That's why it's so crucial that we learn to trust God's vision for our lives and to throw perfectionism out the window. How much better are the plans of the one who created you than your own plans for your life?

KEY VERSES:
"Look at the birds of the air; they do not sow or reap or store away in barns, and yet your heavenly Father feeds them. Are you not much more valuable than they?"
Matthew 6:26

"Humble yourselves, therefore, under God's mighty hand, that he may lift you up in due time. Cast all your anxiety on him because he cares for you."
1 Peter 5:6-7

REFLECTION QUESTIONS:

+ Where have you been looking for value in your life? Is your value placed in what you've accomplished or the things at which you hope to be successful?

+ Have you lacked trust in God's vision for your life? If so, what makes you feel like your plans are better in your own hands than in His?

DAY 2

Do you ever get so zoned-in to something that the person sitting right next to you could be screaming your name and you still wouldn't even notice them? Have you ever treated God the same way? Lauren shares, "I ran after my desire for success, not minding that I was pushing myself further and further away from those around me and from the heart of God." Why is it so easy to tune out everyone around us (including God) in order to do what we want, but when God asks us to spend time with Him, those distractions come rushing back and we are unable to focus on Him? So many of us get so afraid of not achieving our goals that we ignore and hide them. We feel this need to achieve everything on our own, because we think it means we gain all the credit—or we lose the glory, and the blame is only on us when we fail. It can be spun both ways. But what would it look like for us to give our dreams and goals to our community rather than isolating ourselves? It may look like shared help and shared glory or even shared failure and shared blame.

What would it look like for you to share your goals and dreams with God and the community around you? It may mean asking for help or praying for new revelations. It may mean giving up time that could be spent focused on cranking out work, but the result could be having someone join you in your journey toward your goals. Community is meant to build you up and support you, to celebrate when you achieve your goals or when your goals shift or change. Community is ultimately meant to bring us closer to achieving goals rather than distract us from them. Spend time this week asking the Lord to help shift your heart away from competition and into sharing those goals with Him and your community. The sacrifice you might have to make to invite community into your dreams will be worth it when you achieve your dreams and have people to celebrate with you!

KEY VERSES:
"Not only so, but we also glory in our sufferings, because we know that suffering produces perseverance; perseverance, character; and character, hope. And hope does not put us to shame, because God's love has been poured out into our hearts through the Holy Spirit, who has been given to us."
Romans 5:3-5

"You have searched me, LORD, and you know me. You know when I sit and when I rise; you perceive my thoughts from afar. You discern my going out and my lying down; you are familiar with all my ways. Before a word is on my tongue you, LORD, know it completely. You hem me in behind and before, and you lay your hand upon me."
Psalms 139:1-5

REFLECTION QUESTIONS:
+ Lauren shares, "I ran after my desire for success, not minding that I was pushing myself further and further away from those around me and from the heart of God." Has chasing after a goal or a dream isolated you from community and the heart of God? What are you sacrificing for the sake of success?

Whether we realize it or not, our day is filled with desires. We desire to wear this instead of that, we desire a pizza for lunch rather than salad, desire the shoes the girl sitting next to us in class is wearing, desire a relationship like Cece and Schmidt's on New Girl. . . we are constantly desiring things all day long. But do these daily desires always align with God's desires for us?

When we start chasing God's heart, these same daily desires shift from being a lifelong comparison game to a constant celebration of Him. Instead of desiring the life of the people we stalk on Instagram, instead of being jealous of the godly gifts someone else has—we begin to celebrate and appreciate them. Do you tend to lean toward jealousy within your desires? Does this same jealousy rule your dreams for your own life?

Lauren talks about her strong desire for the perfect corner-office job as an editor and how that strong desire caused her to lose focus of what God asked of her daily. Your desire could be rooted in something the world affirms is good: success, money, fitness, beauty, the list goes on. But attaining these material things often leads us into jealousy or creates in us another desire bigger than our souls can afford or catch up to. What if these desires shifted to the simple desire to glorify God in everything we do? When our daily desire shifts to glorifying Him, our heart is always content and we learn how to align with His purposes.

KEY VERSES:
"In his pride the wicked man does not seek him; in all his thoughts there is no room for God."
Psalms 10:4

"May he give you the desire of your heart and make all your plans succeed."
Psalms 20:4

REFLECTION QUESTIONS:
+ When you are truly chasing God's heart, your desires for your life will align with His desires for you. What parts of your dreams have been rooted in selfishness or are distant from your relationship with Him? How could God reshape your dreams when you bring them back to Him?

In college, everything revolves around our choice of major. Our friends, our classes, our extracurricular activities, and even our general campus experience all have to do with our major. Even people who are declared as undecided feel the pressure to fill that hole with a major. The funny thing about this is that most people don't even go into the career field they studied in college. They may start off that way, but eventually they tend to gravitate towards something completely different. And that's okay!

Sometimes college makes us feel like we need to have everything paved out for the rest of our lives. Our dream career has to be the one we decided on at age eighteen. The pressure of planning for the future tends to put up blinders to the little joys of everyday life. We get so focused on the end goal that we rush past potential friends or clubs that could add value to our lives. But if the ultimate dream job rarely ever pans out for us, why do we keep such a laser-sharp focus on it? Why do we allow it to distract us from the daily gifts God gives us?

What if the small, everyday moments can lead you to an even bigger destiny than the one you're planning for yourself? The one person you met who isn't the same major could become your best friend, your ultimate cheerleader and supporter in life, who constantly reminds you of what God says about you. That summer internship that has nothing to do with the ultimate dream could become your passion, eventually leading to a different career path which fits you better than you could have ever imagined.

Sometimes the small things lead into bigger things and sometimes the small things stay small. But God works in silent and mysterious ways. Let Him show you how His gifts can bless you in the here and now, without worrying about their degree of usefulness later.

KEY VERSES:
"Yet you, LORD, are our Father. We are the clay, you are the potter; we are all the work of your hand."
Isaiah 64:8

REFLECTION QUESTIONS:
+ Do you need to fixate more on God's everyday gifts for you rather than your ultimate dream? How might these small moments bring you closer to God's bigger destiny?

CAROLINE

BELMONT UNIVERSITY
PUBLIC RELATIONS
SOPHOMORE

When Pain Has A Purpose

WALKING WITH THE LORD THROUGH THE WILDERNESS

After coming home from a long day of teaching four-year-olds how
to swim, I plopped down on the couch with my mom and turned on a
long-anticipated episode of The Bachelorette. I was enjoying a relaxing
evening during the summer after a very stressful first year of college.
My phone lit up, telling me that my best friend Morgan was calling, but
I didn't answer because watching Rachel's one-on-one date was more
important at the time. Two seconds after declining the call, I received a
text from her mom telling me to call her. My heart started racing as my
mind wandered to every possible worst-case scenario.

"We need you to come over. Morgan needs you. Zach committed
suicide."

My whole body went numb. I felt paralyzed. I vaguely heard my parents
arguing across the house about how they didn't want me driving myself
since I was in shock, but it just sounded like ringing.

"Blessed are those who mourn, for they will be comforted."
Matthew 5:4

Picture your typical redneck who's obsessed with his Ram truck,
country music, and Mountain Dew. That's my friend Zach. Every time
we hung out, whether it was at the mall or a country concert, he was
the life of the party. Above all, he was one of the most selfless people
I had ever met, who always put everyone else's needs before his own.
I had known him since my junior year of high school, but we didn't
really become close until my freshman year of college. Even then,
we weren't close enough to hang out one-on-one, but we still had a
good relationship. Six months before he passed, his younger brother
Alex died from adrenoleukodystrophy, a rare and deadly genetic brain
disorder. Alex and Zach weren't just brothers—they were best friends. I
had never witnessed a bond as strong as the one they shared. The loss

of Alex took such a toll on Zach, it was like a part of him was lost, and ultimately that pain consumed him.

I felt every emotion in the book: I was glad he was reunited with Alex in heaven, sad for his family and friends, mad that he would do this to himself and the people around him, but mostly regretful. I knew deep down there was nothing I could've done personally, but I couldn't help but feel like there was. I wished we were closer, and constantly blamed myself for that. I wished we went to Buffalo Wild Wings, just the two of us, like we had always planned. I wished we took more pictures. I wished I reached out more.

That summer I poured myself into my faith and my church. I attended every Sunday service, morning prayer, and student event. Through all the darkness I had faced the past few weeks, I knew God was a light. My relationship with Him grew tremendously, and I ended up getting re-baptized. Throughout the entire summer, I was surrounded by encouraging people who were not only there for me emotionally, but also helped me draw closer to God and rely on His plan. I knew in my spirit that God would use the pain I was feeling in the aftermath of Zach's death to help others and be a walking testimony.

"Even though I walk through the darkest valley, I will fear no evil, for you are with me; your rod and your staff, they comfort me."
Psalm 23:4

As the summer came to a close, I was dreading going back to college. My freshman year wasn't the easiest, and I was scared I was just going to re-live the difficulties. I was already going into the semester confused about my major and considering transferring. At the same time, I had become closer to God than I'd ever been, and I was comfortable. My community at home helped me get through the loss of Zach, and those people had faithfully walked with me throughout my journey with Christ. I was afraid of losing that.

Once I got back to college, I thought I had to pretend like everything over the summer didn't happen. People wouldn't talk to me about it, and I couldn't separate the people who knew about it from the ones who didn't. I found myself talking about Zach way more than usual, and bringing him up in simple conversations. Then I'd tear myself up about it because my friends back home seemed to be fully recovered. I was broken, but I felt like I had to put on a mask for people.

After my friend had convinced me to go to counseling, I accepted the fact that I was going through a lot. I started feeling better about Zach, but worse about everything else. Every little thing would put me over the edge; from not finding the right pair of shoes for sorority recruitment, to a parking ticket, to being afraid of losing people. I would let one small event affect my entire day, then week, then month. I felt like I was alone in a wilderness, constantly being attacked by whatever life decided to throw at me that day. I ended up having mental breakdowns daily, and never wanted to leave my bed. I wasn't going to church because I was constantly getting scheduled to work at the same time and I wasn't spending time with God because I told myself I was too busy, which only caused more pain and guilt. I was going through the daily motions: going to class, working at my job, and then heading straight back to the comfort of my own bed, not wanting to see or talk to anyone. The volatility of my emotions had reached an all-time high, and I didn't know how to control them.

"Weeping may stay for the night, but rejoicing comes in the morning."
Psalm 30:5

By the grace of God, I was finally not scheduled to work one random Tuesday night. The church I attend in Nashville called The Belonging Co meets regularly on Tuesday nights. I somehow managed to get myself out of bed and go to church for the first time in months. God knew I was going, and knew exactly what I needed to hear. My pastor gave a sermon on wilderness, the very word that summed up exactly what I was feeling. I had always viewed a season of emptiness as a punishment, a period of waiting while everyone around me was growing and fulfilling their purpose. The pastor explained that God isn't punishing us by having us wander through the wilderness, but rather He is preparing us for the destiny that He has perfectly designed for us.

She said, "God doesn't put challenges in our lives so He can learn something about us. He knows us fully. He puts them in our lives so we can learn things about ourselves."

Even if it doesn't make any sense in the moment, He always gives us what we need at the right time and in the right place. We complain and whine about having to go through difficulties, but it's God's training for us. When we throw out the season of wilderness, we never learn how to prepare for the season ahead.

"Therefore I am now going to allure her; I will lead her into the wilderness and speak tenderly to her."
Hosea 2:14

God is luring us to come into the wilderness, and in that season He will speak tenderly to us. God's not mad at us or disciplining us. He's saying, I need to tell you who you are and affirm your identity. You're broken and wanting outside forces to make you feel better, but unless I tell you who you are, you will never be able to fully sustain your destiny. He will not only speak tenderly to us, but He will also restore us and give blessing back to us.

As the worship band began to play and I raised my arms in surrender, tears streamed down my face, washing away my makeup. I had let outside forces get in the way of my relationship with God. I had spent an entire summer serving and building a relationship with Jesus, but I had let it slip right through my fingers. I had convinced myself I was healed from losing Zach, because my friends back home seemed to be healed. I looked at other people's journeys and compared myself even though my journey is different than theirs. My journey was hand-crafted by God specifically for me. I realized that in order to fully emerge from the brokenness I was feeling, I had to give every ounce of myself to God. He wanted me to turn back around and face Him, instead of wallowing in my pain.

As I questioned how I should better focus myself on God, I started reading Jesus Calling. Digging into my faith for the first time in months, the first line I read said: "I, the Creator of the universe, am the most creative Being imaginable. I will not leave you circling in deeply rutted paths. Instead, I will lead you along fresh trails of adventure, revealing to you things you did not know. Stay in communication with Me. Follow My guiding Presence."

God couldn't have been any clearer. I hadn't remained focused and faithful to God as I spent an entire semester in the wilderness, constantly making wrong turns and getting lost. What's worse is that I knew I hadn't put God first, and I didn't do anything about it. But He opened my eyes and showed me that the mess of emotions which had overwhelmed me all semester were signs that I wasn't fully recovered from Zach's death and didn't turn to God to heal my emotional pain. I will never be able to just get over Zach's passing, but I realized it's okay to not be okay sometimes.

"Consider it pure joy, my brothers and sisters, whenever you face trials of many kinds, because you know that the testing of your faith produces perseverance."
James 1:2-3

When we first enter a wilderness season, we experience all these emotions about being stuck there. We compare our faith journey to others' faith journeys, and if we see an imbalance, we convince ourselves there's something wrong with us. Or more often than not, we'll downplay our emotions and tell ourselves that we need to just "tough it out."

Remember recess during elementary school? We'd push and shove each other for a turn on the swings, wait impatiently to be next on the monkey bars, or chase a cute boy in an epic game of tag. But what would happen if we accidentally fell while running around? Chances are the teacher would say something like, "You'll be okay, just tough it out." In the book Girl Meets Change, Kristen Strong discusses our emotions when change arises and writes: "We secretly wish we were more robot than flesh and heart so we could reprogram our brains and bodies to just get over it. We need to be okay with not getting over it and give ourselves permission to feel the upheaval."

We shouldn't have to tough it out. God didn't make us robots, He breathed life into us. He gave us flesh and heart, which feel all sorts of things. When Jesus takes us into a place of isolation, where our emotions become fully exposed, it's so we will hear His voice above everything else. Jesus doesn't hold up a measuring stick and tell us that our pain is lesser than the pain of the person sitting next to us. Instead, He comforts us. He puts His arms around us as we weep at His feet. We all experience pain and suffering, but in our seasons of wilderness we must push away what the enemy meant for evil and ask God what the purpose of this pain is and how we will become better equipped for the destiny he has planned ahead.

When we don't allow God to take us into that wilderness, we miss out on a destiny that's greater than we could ever imagine. His destiny for us is bigger and better than we think. We never know where He's going to take us, maybe places we never thought we'd end up, but the wilderness prepares us for what's around the corner. I didn't know how, and honestly still haven't quite figured it out, but I knew God would use this season of pain and emptiness for a purpose. I had never looked at experiencing wilderness as a positive change before. Positivity in itself is hard enough for me, let alone choosing to look at this season in an optimistic light. I had been so focused on every little negative thing in my life that I didn't think about God using this season as a lesson to lean on Him no matter what. He puts us through these paths of uncertainty so that we may rely on Him more. So when pain, doubt, questioning, and wilderness arise, we shouldn't shove it aside. We should surrender and embrace it with our arms wide open, crying out to Jesus because He's the only one who can fill our emptiness.

"See, I am doing a new thing! Now it springs up; do you not perceive it? I am making a way in the wilderness and streams in the wasteland."
Isaiah 43:19

I still have a hard time relying 100% on God and His plan, but I try and look at the problems that arise in a more positive light. Deep down I know Jesus has a plan for me greater than I could ever imagine, and in order to reach that I have to accept the wilderness with open arms. When I start to compare myself and my life to those around me, I try to think back to my wilderness season, and remind myself that my journey is my own.

There are moments in college that can feel like a wilderness. We've been thrown into an entirely new environment, with complete strangers, and may have no clear direction on what to do or where to go. But God uses a time like college to strengthen who we are and clarify our purpose in life. It's important that we learn to focus on the wonders this season provides, and reflect on why God has placed us there, so we can discover more of His purpose for each of our beautiful lives.

KEY VERSES:

Matthew 5:4
Psalm 23:4
Psalm 30:5
Hosea 2:14
James 1:2-3
Isaiah 43:19

DISCUSSION QUESTIONS:

+ How have you responded to unexpected moments of pain in your life? Do these moments leave you questioning the goodness of God?

+ Is there pain in your life that you've stopped sharing with others? Why have you suppressed these feelings? Have you let others' journeys of healing impact the way you view your own?

+ Caroline reminds us, "We shouldn't have to tough it out. God didn't make us robots, He breathed life into us. He gave us flesh and heart, which feel all sorts of things." Do you often feel the temptation to toughen up and move on from hardships? Why do you think the enemy wants you to suppress your emotions? Why do you think the Lord wants you to feel the depths of them?

+ God isn't punishing us by having us wander through the wilderness, but rather He is preparing us for the destiny that He has perfectly designed for us. Have you ever viewed a season of wilderness as a season of punishment? How is God using your pain for a purpose in your life?

+ Do you have a friend who needs to see purpose in their pain? How can you highlight the voice of God for them in the midst of a really difficult season?

DEVOTIONALS

CONTRIBUTOR: *Ashley Albers*

DAY 1

Pain is an inevitable part of life that can feel messy, broken, and unbearable. We will face heartaches, confusion, and find ourselves asking the question: why, God? At the same time life also brings joy, laughter, and smiles. Days where our purpose and pain come full circle. Relationships come and go. Friends walk with us and then walk away. People leave without explanation. Tragedies happen. Pain never gets easier, but it can always lead us closer to the Lord. When we face hardships, we have the choice to either run farther from God or to run straight to His open arms.

Our human nature often leads us to shut down when the pain gets too intense. But delving into our emotions can be an extraordinary catalyst for change and deeper intimacy not only with the Lord, but also with the people around us. In our most painful moments, we need to keep our community closer than ever. Take comfort in the ones who love you, take solace in the Lord, and accept the pain as a way to grow stronger and wiser.

KEY VERSES:
"Even though I walk through the darkest valley, I will fear no evil, for you are with me; your rod and your staff, they comfort me."
Psalm 23:4

REFLECTION QUESTIONS:
+ How have you responded to unexpected moments of pain in your life? Do these moments leave you questioning the goodness of God?

+ Is there pain in your life that you've stopped sharing with others? Why have you suppressed these feelings? Have you let others' journeys of healing impact the way you view your own?

In today's American society, women often feel a pressure to be "all things to all people." Unrealistic expectations about how our lives should appear constantly bombard us. We have all dealt with expectations for the way we should look and the way we should act—expectations for the perfect life, perfect relationship, perfect career, and an even more perfect Instagram (as if that even exists). These impossible standards also tell us not to crumble when everything else seems to be falling apart, making us feel like we have no choice except to put up walls and keep everybody out.

This pressure to be "strong" isn't in line with God's heart for us. God doesn't have unfair expectations of us or ask us to be whole all the time. He wants us to be honest with ourselves and honest with Him so that we can grow closer to Him. When we're willing to be broken before God, His power rests on us and allows Him to start re-shaping our pain and hurt. When pain creeps in, we need to remind ourselves that His arms are the only place we should seek for refuge. He's the only one strong enough to take away the burden of our heartache and heal us completely.

KEY VERSES:
"Blessed are those who mourn, for they will be comforted."
Matthew 5:4

REFLECTION QUESTIONS:
+ Caroline reminds us, "We shouldn't have to tough it out. God didn't make us robots, He breathed life into us. He gave us flesh and heart, which feel all sorts of things." Do you often feel the temptation to toughen up and move on from hardships? Why do you think the enemy wants you to suppress your emotions? Why do you think the Lord wants you to feel the depths of them?

DAY 3

Seasons of wilderness can feel like a punishment rather than a place of purpose. We're so quick to blame others or even blame the Lord when things get tough, assuming God is leaving us or forgot about us just because we're facing trials. Don't even let these thoughts take root in your mind. Every path that we encounter has a purpose. God lets us choose our paths, but He also knows what challenges and victories we will accomplish. He desires for us to take paths that will lead us into His arms and grow our faith.

When pain arises and you find yourself stumbling through the wilderness, struggling to take the next step, keep your heart set on the Lord's good intentions and have faith that whatever you are going through will build you back up in God's image. Stay close to the Lord and look for His purpose in the wilderness.

KEY VERSES:
"Therefore I am now going to allure her; I will lead her into the wilderness and speak tenderly to her."
Hosea 2:14

"Consider it pure joy, my brothers and sisters, whenever you face trials of many kinds, because you know that the testing of your faith produces perseverance."
James 1:2-3

REFLECTION QUESTIONS:
+ God isn't punishing us by having us wander through the wilderness, but rather He is preparing us for the destiny that He has perfectly designed for us. Have you ever viewed a season of wilderness as a season of punishment? How is God using your pain for a purpose in your life?

DAY 4

Who helps you see the purpose in your pain? Maybe you find yourself calling your mom or dad when you're having a bad day. Maybe it's your friend who lives down the hall or a mentor from high school who always helps clarify your circumstances. Other believers have the ability to highlight the movements of God that we might not be able to see on our own.

In the same way these friends have guided you, God can use you as an instrument of peace in the lives of people around you. It's great to be a friend who will meet others in their brokenness, but it's even better (and more purposeful) to help others see God's desire to redeem their brokenness. Let the Lord use you in the lives of your friends and family. Be available for them when they are struggling with emotional pain, and remind them of God's goodness despite their circumstances. You can be the one to help bring them out of the wilderness and back into the Lord's light.

KEY VERSES:
"See, I am doing a new thing! Now it springs up; do you not perceive it? I am making a way in the wilderness and streams in the wasteland."
Isaiah 43:19

REFLECTION QUESTIONS:
+ Do you have a friend who needs to see purpose in their pain? How can you highlight the voice of God for them in the midst of a really difficult season?

GRACIE

APPALACHIAN STATE UNIVERSITY
COMMUNICATION STUDIES
FRESHMAN

Resting In God

HOW SEASONS OF STILLNESS CAN PROVIDE CLARITY

In American culture we are taught in order to be successful we have to be in charge of our own lives. In the kingdom of God, we are asked to be counter-cultural—to turn our backs on our culture and yield to God's plan. In my experience, I believed that I had enough faith to do life on my own. I mean I had to be doing something right, right? I had heard the stories, declared my faith, and I was itching to get out into the world and share the light of Christ. I knew that I needed God, but I thought it would be okay for me to take the driver's seat for a little while. I thought I was in control of my life. However, life has a funny way of getting in the way of comfort. It seems to me that just when I'm comfortable, life changes. It seems like every time I'm starting to get good at doing things on my own, God reminds me that I do, in fact, need Him.

2017 was arguably the most transformative year of my life. On January 1st, I rang in the year by burying my father, who passed away after nearly a decade of battling ALS. It was the year of my high school graduation. It was my acceptance into college. It was my first semester on my own. Everything was different. Everything was changing right before my eyes. There was not a single constant in my life other than God's love for me. I didn't falter in the early months of 2017 like you'd expect. In fact, I did quite the opposite. I threw my trust into the Lord and began building a life I thought would bring glory to both my earthly father and my heavenly father. The season of life after my father's death came as a gift. It seemed as though through his passing he had left me a final present: a blank slate.

I kept myself busy because I was afraid that if I stopped, I would suddenly find myself in a dark place that I couldn't come back from. So I made a conscious decision not to stop. I kept adding new pieces to my life to distract myself from the hurt lying inside my heart. My plan was perfect, or so I thought. I thought if I didn't allow sadness to enter my life my problems may just go away, so I left no time for myself to be sad. I arrived at college with a heart full of expectations which I believed would get me through the next four years. Not surprisingly, it only took about a week for me to realize that all the things I had expected college to fix for me couldn't be fixed by simply moving away from home.

College is weird. It's a transitional period of life. Everything is so new and unknown. You hear all the time that college will be a time of discovery and reinvention. And in theory, this is awesome—a time to create a new self. But in reality, leaving pieces of yourself behind and adopting new ones is really hard. You are quite literally creating a new identity for yourself. I mean, why not? It's a blank slate. While it can be exciting for a while to create something new, at some point you realize that you have to take a step back. You have to look at the person you are leaving behind and decide if you truly want to let her go. You have to acknowledge that maybe you need fixing after all; that you aren't always okay.

I realized that I didn't know who I was. I thought I did. I had been labeled with identities my whole life. People associated me with strength, leadership, and joy. I clung to these labels and rooted my actions in them. I thought I knew what to do with them. When I entered college, I realized those labels I was clinging to had disappeared. It wasn't that I didn't possess qualities of these characteristics, it was that nobody knew about them. People only knew what I chose to tell them. The sheer amount of options I had in front of me was overwhelming. I came to the conclusion that I couldn't just hide under my labels anymore. I had to accept the person I wanted to be and move on with who I was becoming. This was the beginning of a season in which I felt lonely and lost. Although I had once thought I had a foundation built on concrete, with every passing day it seemed to feel more and more like sinking sand.

Tired of feeling the weight of these emotions, I went out searching for answers. At first I sought comfort through conversations with friends. I would confide in them, hoping that once I said what was hurting me out loud, I would feel better. They would listen and give me supportive feedback, but it was never quite the fix I was looking for. When that didn't work, I thought maybe I needed professional help so I sought out a counselor. Surely a professional would be able to tell me what I was trying to find. After a few sessions I realized talking to this person was still not giving me the answer I was seeking, but rather putting more questions on my heart. My next step was to seek answers in the church.

I attend a non-denominational church called The Heart in Boone, North Carolina. I love this place. Every Sunday we gather in a high school auditorium and praise the Lord with musical worship followed by a teaching sermon by our pastor, Jason English. This past semester we have been in an extended teaching on the Biblical identity and lifestyle of the church. The past couple of sermons had been beautiful, heartfelt, and exactly what I thought I needed to hear. But then one Sunday, the sermon was about Sabbath rest. I remember sitting in my chair in the auditorium thinking, why on earth would I rest? That is literally all I am doing. I have nothing to do. I don't know who I am. The last thing I need is more rest. I need something to keep me busy. I need to do something to figure out who I am. I left that Sunday morning annoyed and with an ignorant heart.

Days passed, and the sermon kept coming up in casual conversation with my friends. One of them described it as "one of those sermons that stops you dead in your tracks and forces you to reevaluate yourself." Hearing this made me feel alone again. I still had no answers—only questions—and I couldn't see how resting could possibly be the answer to my problem. I found myself in a low place, both spiritually and mentally. Tired of feeling empty and confused, I made the decision to go back and listen to Jason's sermon. Maybe if I listened again, I would hear the part that was making everybody else feel something. I needed to feel something.

The first words I heard were: "Rest is not the same thing as doing nothing." Immediately I realized I had been wrong all along. The point was made clearer through a story Jason told about taking a silent retreat for five days. No music. No Netflix episodes. No noise or distractions. Nothing to pass the time, just five days of being with yourself. If you think about it, that's honestly terrifying. What do you do when all the distractions are eliminated and it's only you and the Lord? What if you realize you don't actually like the person you are trying to be? What if, when you stop, you realize that the pain of the world is real and you're very much stuck in it? I realized that I am painfully good at the art of distracting myself. I felt my eyes open to this reality that every day is a cycle, a forced race with a finish line that doesn't exist. When we have to stop, we break down. We can't seem to make the conscious decision to rest on our own. We have to realize that this sprint we are running is draining us. We aren't built to be running our whole lives. We need rest, and when we inevitably don't get it, we'll be left gasping for breath and collapsing.

"In returning and rest you shall be saved; in quietness and in trust shall be your strength. But you were unwilling."
Isaiah 30:15 NKJV

Rest is a difficult concept to grasp, especially in our day-to-day lives when work, friends, family, and school all compete for our attention in a never-ending cycle. These things are not inherently bad, and are in fact really amazing gifts from God. But it would be ridiculous for us to keep running through that never-ending cycle, ignoring the signs indicating that we are exhausted. Even more so, it would be outrageous to believe that we are above needing rest. In the beginning God created time for rest. He saw that His works were good and He wanted to sit in that goodness. Rest is not supposed to feel like a burden. It's designed to bless the mind with the space and peace it needs to carry on. He wants to be with us in it. He wants to give us time for peace.

God isn't impractical. He knows that we will ultimately struggle giving up control to Him. I was trying to find answers to questions, but I could have saved myself from worrying so much if I had actually taken time to ask God and rest until I found an answer. I sat there in my weakness and thought I was the exception. However, I'm not the exception, nobody is. The Lord is gracious—He knows that we won't always seek Him first, but when we finally do look for Him, He isn't going to turn away from us.

"Yet the LORD longs to be gracious to you; therefore he will rise up to show you compassion. For the LORD is a God of justice. Blessed are all who wait for him!
Isaiah 30:18

He will be gracious to me. He will wait for me. Isn't that incredible? He will wait forever for me to realize that I'm weaker when I am alone. I can't do it all. I need a place to lie down, and when I do, His arms will be open wide.

"I lie down and sleep; I wake again, for the Lord sustains me."
Psalm 3:5

To echo the words of my pastor, rest is not the same thing as doing nothing. When babies fall asleep they are naturally most comfortable in the arms of their parents. They don't know if they will wake up or not. But somehow in their little experience, they still know that these people aren't going to drop them. They are resting in the arms of the ones who created them, who love them. I wanted to rebel from that love. I thought I could rest in myself and be perfectly fine. But resting in yourself is lonely and draining. I actually don't believe that it's truly possible to rest solely in yourself. You end up needing rest from your rest and that's ridiculous. Here I am tiring myself out, when my Father is sitting right there, waiting for me, saying, "Lie down. Be still. Rest. I've got you." Rest is being comfortable with not having all the answers. The answers aren't found within us anyway, they're found in God alone. I needed to make peace with that. Because when I made my peace with it, I found what I was looking for.

Even with all that being said, how do we make time to rest in the Lord? Jason said in his sermon, "We as humans take time and make space, but God takes space and makes time." We have to allow ourselves to make space and time for God. I took this idea and ran with it.

On a sunny day in November I decided to take a hike by myself on the parkway. I didn't exactly know what I was going to do with this time, but I was praying that it would reveal itself to me when I got there—wherever "there" was. I drove out to a grassy trail, parked my car, and started walking. I didn't know where I was going when I started walking, and I liked it that way. It felt good to finally be taking time to do something with no agenda, just walking with myself and the Lord. I found a spot off the beaten path and began writing, feeling a familiar relief through expressing myself in words. When I read it back to myself I realized that I had written a letter to myself and God.

"The Lord replied, 'My Presence will go with you, and I will give you rest.'"
Exodus 33:14

I wrote:

I'm sitting here on the side of a hill in the mountains of North Carolina. I came here alone to rest. After I parked I walked down a hill. I wanted to be somewhere secluded, and off the beaten path. I couldn't stop noticing the grassy topped hills on the side of the trail to my right. I wanted to go and sit over on the hill. So I veered off the trail. I noticed there was a creek and a fence keeping me from reaching the grassy hill where I wanted to be. I could have stopped and turned around but I couldn't. Something was calling me to go farther. I feel like I haven't done a lot of that lately. I have been watching from afar trying to reach the place I wanted to be simply by watching. But it doesn't work that way. I'm sitting just past the fence at the bottom of the hills. Those hills look like my life. They are blocking me from seeing the other side. I'm in the gully of a valley. It's getting colder. I can feel the chill in my bones. But perhaps that's what I need. I need to feel cold before I can feel warm again. I'm here for the long haul. I'm in it for the end game.

"In the wilderness prepare the way for the LORD; make straight in the desert a highway for our God. Every valley shall be raised up, every mountain and hill made low, the rough ground shall become level, the rugged places a plain. And the glory of the LORD will be revealed, and all people will see it together. For the mouth of the LORD has spoken."
Isaiah 40:3-8

"You are my hiding place; You will protect me from trouble and surround me with songs of deliverance."
Psalm 32:7

I've read these verses and this letter to myself perhaps a dozen times now. Each time I read them, I'm reminded that when we intentionally create space and time for God, we position ourselves to receive clarity about our lives. I know that we can't all literally go 15 minutes down the road and sit in valleys on the sides of mountains. But we can all make some space where we are to dive into the Word and silence of the Lord. When I finally took time to rest, I was able to see that I don't always cross the creek or jump the fence because I get too worried that if I do, I'll be lost. But the beautiful truth is that the Lord is on the other side—and there is no place in this world safer for me than the place God calls me to be.

Rest looks different for different people. Not every single moment of rest is going to provide a life-altering product. In our culture, patience is a fleeting virtue—partly because we have access to so much so quickly. But the Bible isn't Google and God isn't Siri. We can't expect immediate answers from Him. We have to carve out space and time to listen and really hear the words we need. Rest looks a lot like faith in the sense that it is a journey. Sometimes you have to look back and reflect on past times of rest before God reveals the answer to your current problem. Different experiences will provide clarity in different times. My rest comes when I'm sitting by myself drinking coffee, taking a drive, or walking. Other people find rest in their own ways, preferring to lay in their own thoughts in a comfortable place or enjoying time with friends or family.

Rest isn't cut and dry. It's fluid and it can be what you need it to be. In order to cultivate a relationship, you have to spend time with the other person. I believe that when we rest with God, we are spending quality time with Him regardless of the form of rest we choose. When we get to know Him better He in turn will help us learn more about ourselves. I promise the more you pour into Him, the more He will pour out into you.

"You did not choose me, but I chose you and appointed you so that you might go and bear fruit—fruit that will last—and so that whatever you ask in my name the Father will give you."
John 15:16

Rest is not the same thing as doing nothing. I am not doing nothing right now. I am resting in the spirit of the Lord. I'm not perfect, by any means, but I am in a season of acceptance. I am no longer giving myself the power to control my own life. I am no longer letting labels define me. I am no longer looking for answers. I now know that kind of power is exhausting and it's meant for the Father who created us. I'm resting. I want to be able to hear Him when He calls. Where the Lord calls me, I will go. Where the Lord yields, I will yield. I'm giving it all up, because I know that the power of Christ is assuring. I will rest in the steadfast love of my Father, who loves me forever and ever.

KEY VERSES:

Isaiah 30:15
Isaiah 30:18
Psalm 3:5
Exodus 33:14
Isaiah 40:3-8
Psalm 32:7
John 15:16

DISCUSSION QUESTIONS:

+ What do you try to control most in your life? Why have you held onto this area so tightly?

+ Starting college creates the scary but cool opportunity to create a new "label" for yourself. What is this label? Have you been so distracted creating this new identity for yourself that you've missed who God is calling you to be?

+ When you feel the need to rest, do you find yourself trying to distract yourself instead? What do you use as a distraction and how is this pulling you away from God?

+ Gracie reminds us that "rest is not the same thing as doing nothing." How have you been spending your time of rest? In what ways can you reshape these moments to be a more intentional pursuit of intimacy with Jesus?

+ Like Gracie, do you need to take a moment this week to do something with no agenda? Is there an answer you have been waiting for that could be heard or better understood when you create uncontrolled space for God to speak?

DEVOTIONALS

CONTRIBUTOR: Madison Gattis

DAY 1

Many of us have experienced the fear of losing control over our own lives. We fail to rest in the Lord because we are too busy trying to control what our lives look like on a day-to-day basis. As Gracie comes to realize in her story, only God is fully in control over our lives. The sooner we can realize that and learn to trust Him with that control, the better our relationship with God will become.

Obviously, this is much easier said than done. The best place to start is by first identifying the area in your life in which you have struggled to fully give control over to God. Maybe it's school, maybe it's relationships, or one of the many other things that are out of our human control. Once you identify that area, see if you can figure out why you've tried to hold onto this area of your life so tightly. Once you uncover the reason behind your need to control that area of your life, pray over it. Ask God to help you let go of control and give it over to Him. After all, only He can have full control and His plan for our lives is far better than the plans we make for ourselves. This will allow you to rest in the peace of knowing He has a plan and has taken control over your fears. Be still in the comfort of knowing that God is in control, always providing for you exactly what you need.

KEY VERSES:
"In returning and rest you shall be saved; in quietness and in trust shall be your strength. But you were unwilling."
Isaiah 30:15 NKJV

REFLECTION QUESTIONS:
+ What do you try to control most in your life? Why have you held on to this area so tightly?

When you think about your identity, is it currently found in God or in something else? Focus your prayer today on identifying where you are finding your identity and how you can place more of it in God. Often we become so entangled in what we think our identity should be that we overlook who God is telling us we are. This becomes dangerous because misplacing our truest self will always leave us feeling empty and unsatisfied. We forget who God calls us to be and end up lost with no direction, defined by a false label that we've given ourselves. Sometimes we give ourselves these labels because we believe that the way others perceive us is the truth of who we are. Don't worry though, there's good news! We can rest in our identity as daughters of God, knowing that He steadfastly loves and values each of us as unique individuals. We don't have to try to be somebody else or act a certain way in order to gain His love. There's no pressure—rest in knowing that you are made perfectly in His image.

KEY VERSES:
"Yet the LORD longs to be gracious to you; therefore he will rise up to show you compassion. For the LORD is a God of justice. Blessed are all who wait for him!"
Isaiah 30:18

"The Lord replied, 'My Presence will go with you, and I will give you rest.'"
Exodus 33:14

REFLECTION QUESTIONS:
+ Starting college creates the scary but cool opportunity to create a new "label" for yourself. What is this label? Have you been so distracted creating this new identity for yourself that you've missed who God is calling you to be?

DAY 3

Resting in the Lord is difficult to do in our fast-paced American society. Like Gracie describes, taking time to stop and rest goes against everything we have been trained to do. But even when we do finally stop, we have to be careful to remember that a lack of activity is not the same as intentionally setting apart time to spend with God. The key is to be intentional when spending time with God. Just sitting somewhere quiet with no one else around and waiting for Him to speak to you is a great way to ensure quality time with the Lord. Sometimes He will speak to you in these moments—when you didn't even believe He was listening to what you needed. The Lord knows our hearts so well, always ready for us when we realize we need Him more than we need ourselves. Don't be afraid to rest in knowing how well He knows and loves you.

KEY VERSES:
"I lie down and sleep; I wake again, for the Lord sustains me."
Psalm 3:5

"In the wilderness prepare the way for the LORD; make straight in the desert a highway for our God. Every valley shall be raised up, every mountain and hill made low, the rough ground shall become level, the rugged places a plain. And the glory of the LORD will be revealed, and all people will see it together. For the mouth of the LORD has spoken."
Isaiah 40:3-8

REFLECTION QUESTIONS:
+ When you feel the need to rest, do you find yourself trying to distract yourself instead? What do you use as a distraction and how is this pulling you away from God?

+ Gracie reminds us that "rest is not the same thing as doing nothing." How have you been spending your time of rest? In what ways can you reshape these moments to be a more intentional pursuit of intimacy with Jesus?

Have you ever stopped your day and done nothing at all except sat down and listened to God? It's extremely difficult, but yet so important. Each of us desperately needs to pay attention and spend time working on our relationship with Him just like we would do in any other relationship. This work requires fighting the desire for task-oriented instant gratification which our society has taught us. It's hard work, but it's one of the best ways to grow a personal relationship with God. He appreciates when we're intentional about spending our time with Him. As Gracie mentioned in her story, rest is a journey just like faith. It's not a box we can just check off after 5 minutes of closing our eyes. We have to pray for rest and spend time developing a way to practice it before we can fully achieve it. That's the beauty of a relationship with God. It requires patience and time to figure out. Stopping your busyness and talking to the Lord with no distractions is incredibly challenging, but you can do it! Pray for Him to reveal things to you about yourself that you never knew. Pray in the name of Jesus that you can find rest and comfort in the Father's heart for you.

KEY VERSES:
"You are my hiding place; You will protect me from trouble and surround me with songs of deliverance."
Romans 8:5
Psalm 32:7

"You did not choose me, but I chose you and appointed you so that you might go and bear fruit—fruit that will last—and so that whatever you ask in my name the Father will give you."
John 15:16

REFLECTION QUESTIONS:
+ Like Gracie, do you need to take a moment this week to do something with no agenda? Is there an answer you have been waiting for that could be heard or better understood when you create uncontrolled space for God to speak?

EMILY

TEXAS A&M UNIVERSITY
BIOMEDICAL ENGINEERING
FRESHMAN

Intimacy With Jesus

LETTING GOD BE YOUR ULTIMATE SOURCE OF FULFILLMENT

If I were to give you a packing list for attending Texas A&M, the very first item would be a pitcher with a water filter. People always told me that Dallas water tasted bad, but let me tell you, Dallas water has nothing on College Station. It tastes—and smells—like it came straight out of the Brazos River.

Recently I was volunteering at a children's ministry in College Station when some of the girls asked to get water. We found the nearest water fountain and after one sip, the sweet third-grader turned to me and complained, "You know, this water doesn't really taste good." I of course agreed. She took another drink and followed up with, "But when you're really thirsty, it doesn't matter all that much."

Isn't it true that when we're really thirsty, we can trick ourselves into settling for whatever happens to be most convenient? We choose whatever will quench our immediate thirst, whatever will provide a temporary relief, even if it will lead to sickness and dehydration a few hours later. We fixate on thinking that the figurative water fountain is our best option because it's the one that we can see. We fight for control and, in doing so, we often miss out on God's best for us. What if we looked a little harder for the spring of life? What if we invested a little more time to find the only one who can not only meet our needs, but satisfy our soul?

"You make known to me the path of life; you will fill me with joy in your presence, with eternal pleasures at your right hand."
Psalm 16:11

I love being around people. Until I had a drastically introverted friend, I simply couldn't comprehend how people became socially tired. Being in marching band in high school fueled my social energy. There was always someone new to talk to or hang out with. Going into college, I was excited to finally live without the constraints of my parents; I could hang out with people any time I wanted. I dreamt of meeting my lifelong friends, the people with whom I would look back on college and recount all of our shared memories. The people I would still want to talk to when we weren't living in the same town. The people who would stand beside me on my wedding day.

Because I was going to such a big school, it seemed like everyone I talked to emphasized the importance of getting involved in a student organization. Texas A&M has eighteen Freshman Leadership Organizations and I figured one of them would be a good fit. While most of my friends applied for two or three, I applied for six. I completed six applications and six interviews, sure that I would get into at least one. The process ultimately ended in an email that read, "Unfortunately, we were not able to place you in a Freshman Leadership Organization." I couldn't believe it. I read the email over and over again. I was sure that a FLO would be the perfect place for me to find the friends I desired. I dreaded the loneliness which I was sure would quickly ensue. I texted my best friend (and roommate) and she told me which FLO she had gotten into—it was not only the one at the top of my list, but it was a community full of strong Christian men and women that I now wouldn't get a chance to join. I was devastated. As I watched her go to her first meeting and retreat, I couldn't help but compare her new opportunity to my failure. She had found her group; she was going to find her bridesmaids while I sat in a dorm room by myself.

I went home the following weekend and had an amazing time with friends that I knew from high school. When I got back to College Station, I listened as my roommate recounted her weekend with her friends from her new organization. Instead of celebrating with joy for my longtime friend, I only felt envious and isolated. I later left the room, and ended up sitting under a tree near my dorm. In tears, I called one of my closest friends from high school, with whom I had just spent the weekend. I laid out my biggest fear at the time: "What if I never make the friends in college like I had in high school?" After some calming down and encouragement—and laughter at how ridiculous I must have looked to students passing by—I went back to my dorm and opened up the book Nothing to Prove by Jennie Allen. I read a line that changed my world more than the rejection email ever could: "Loneliness is meant to be an invitation to draw closer to God."

"For he satisfies the thirsty and fills the hungry with good things."
Psalm 107:9

My friends were my proverbial water fountain. In my foolishness, I wondered why I should look for something better when it seemed like there was a solution right in front of me. It doesn't feel like we need God when we trick ourselves into thinking that the solution in front of us is good enough. The problem was that no number of friends was going to satisfy my deep longing for connection and intimacy. This unmet need for the Holy Spirit was so strong that even if I'd had all the friends in the world, I still would have felt lonely.

Without weekend plans, I was in my dorm a lot more than I thought I would be. Inspired by Jennie Allen's words, I actually opened my Bible. I consistently spent time with the Lord for the first time in my life. As I leaned into Jesus, He leaned into me, just like He promises that He will. I wasn't suddenly okay with loneliness, and I didn't suddenly have friends to hang out with, but I could see God as the fixed horizon in the midst of the storm. I began to crave time spent with the Lord, yearning for His presence in a completely new way. This spiritual filling of my soul was an answer to what I had really been craving: unconditional love, true connection, and deep intimacy.

In my youth I had always shrugged off quiet times, arguing that being alone just "really wasn't my thing." It was difficult for me to feel community with an invisible God, so I turned instead to people, aching for the feeling of someone knowing everything about me and loving me anyway. I was so thirsty for true love that I was willing to settle for earthly love instead of turning to my Father—who not only wholly knows me, but also completely loves me—for void-filling, soul-satisfying living water.

"But whoever drinks the water I give them will never thirst. Indeed, the water I give them will become in them a spring of water welling up to eternal life."
John 4:14

Here's the deal: I'm not perfect. You're not perfect. If we believe that to be true, how can we expect the people in our lives to be? People are going to disappoint us, just like we are going to disappoint them. We have to stop trying to make our community into our Christ. When we make people our saviors, we're setting them up to fail by putting them in a role they were never meant to fulfill. The only one that can ultimately meet our needs is Jesus.

"The LORD will guide you always; he will satisfy your needs in a sun-scorched land and will strengthen your frame. You will be like a well-watered garden, like a spring whose waters never fail."
Isaiah 58:11

If this earth is all there is, the best we can hope for is human connection; although fortunately, it's not. Borrowing an illustration from Francis Chan, this time on Earth is just an aglet to the long, long shoelace of our existence. We were not meant for this world. Heaven is our home. Don't get distracted by the echoes of heaven found in earthly pleasures. If we have a supernatural longing to be satisfied, how could we expect to fulfill that desire with things on this earth? Tom Brady, after winning his fourth Super Bowl, confessed to a journalist that he felt there "has to be more than this." Even with his family, wealth, success, and fame, Tom Brady knew deep within his soul that there is more to life than chasing the world's ever-changing idea of perfection. No amount of success or friends or love or self-improvement ever feels like enough. As we approach the finish line, it moves a little farther out of reach.

Let's run a different race. When the world says to go fill your schedule, go market yourself, go make any kind of connection, let us slow down and rest in God's presence. Life is found in the one who created it. We were made for an intimate relationship with our creator.

"Come to me, all you who are weary and burdened, and I will give you rest. Take my yoke upon you and learn from me, for I am gentle and humble in heart, and you will find rest for your souls."
Matthew 11:28-29

After lots of praying, reading the Bible, crying ugly tears, and spending time with the Lord, I was reminded of a childhood friend who attends Belmont University in Nashville. Before we left for college, she told me all about a nationwide ministry for college women to not only grow deeper in their faith, but also to enjoy a solid, Christ-centered community. She was excited to join once she was at Belmont, and told me to consider it. I went to a Delight worship night after stalking the chapter's Instagram and was immediately welcomed by girls who, although I didn't know it at the time, would later prove to be incredible movie dates, study buddies, lunch companions, and more. I'm so thankful for the community Jesus brought me to, but daily spending time in His presence reminds me that Delight isn't what made me feel whole—He is.

Growing up in a Christian home means I've known the Gospel story for a long time. I could tell you the ABC's of the Roman Road. But having the head knowledge that the God of the universe deeply loves you and pursues you is different from feeling it to your core. The Lord had to take away my water fountain to make me realize that I was missing out on the living water. I traded the spiritual highs of church camp for walking step by step through every day, every decision, and every moment with my perfect, loving Father. Every bit of sleep that I've lost, every tear that I've shed in my brokenness; I wouldn't trade any of it for the growth that I've experienced as a result of consistent time invested in Scripture and prayer.

"Taste and see that the LORD is good; blessed is the one who takes refuge in him. Fear the LORD, you his holy people, for those who fear him lack nothing. The lions may grow weak and hungry, but those who seek the LORD lack no good thing."
Psalm 34:8-10

I encourage you to determine your own water fountain. What are you putting in God's place, hoping it will meet the desires of your heart? When we recognize His sovereignty, we see a God worth making time for. Maybe you've never spent time alone with Jesus. Maybe you're spending meaningful consistent time in His presence. Maybe you're treating that time like a chore that just needs to be checked off a list. Wherever you are, I am praying that your affections would be stirred, and that you would see a new beginning in your walk with Jesus.

Lord, reveal Your goodness to us; remind us of the sweetness of Your presence. There is no water fountain that will satisfy. You are good. You are faithful. You are victorious over every trial and better than any victory. We want to know You, love You, and serve You deeper.

"Better is one day in your court than a thousand elsewhere; I would rather be a doorkeeper in the house of my God than dwell in the tents of the wicked."
Psalm 84:10

KEY VERSES:
Psalm 16:11
Psalm 107:9
John 4:14
Isaiah 58:11
Matthew 11:28-29
Psalm 34:8-10
Psalm 84:10

DISCUSSION QUESTIONS:
+ Share about a time in college when a friend was given an opportunity that you would've wanted. How did this affect the way you saw your circumstances?

+ Emily shares that "no number of friends was going to satisfy [her] deep longing for connection and intimacy with Jesus." Where do you run for immediate satisfaction? Have you let this take the place of intimacy with Jesus? Why?

+ Have you been relying on your friends to be your source of fulfillment in college? How do you need to better balance your communion with Jesus versus time spent in community?

+ A lot of us know that God loves us, but that's different from feeling it deeply in our souls. In what ways are you lacking intimacy in your walk with the Lord? Have you been rushing a relationship or time with Him recently? How might you need to change your quiet time so that it feels less like a chore?

+ How do you need to leave more room for communion with Jesus? How could your life look different if you make the choice to go to Jesus first?

DEVOTIONALS

CONTRIBUTOR: *Carly Rodriguez*

DAY 1

Our hearts crave connection. We desire to feel full, loved, and accepted. Too often we seek worldly organizations, relationships, and titles to fulfill our hearts' greatest desires, while knowing that the satisfaction will only be temporary. In the midst of wanting to belong, rejection will make its way into our lives one way or another, and it can be overwhelmingly painful.

When you do inevitably face rejection, are you going to let bitterness win? Or will you make the choice to live like you are loved by God despite the earthly rejection? It's incredibly natural for our human hearts to seek the quick way out of our emptiness. Instead of spending time in prayer, it would be easier to call a friend, go out of town to escape, or go to that party we have been invited to. But ultimately the only way we can fight against the emptiness is by being still and accepting Christ's daily invitation to pursue Him.

Instead of passively letting our community take the place of intimacy we could experience with Jesus, let's lift our hands high to the Lord and ask Him to fill any empty spaces in our hearts. In the midst of the lonely places, don't forget the simplicity and power of prayer. Our God is everlasting and right at our fingertips.

"The more beauty we find in someone else's journey, the less we'll want to compare it to our own."
Bob Goff

KEY VERSES:
"You make known to me the path of life; you will fill me with joy in your presence, with eternal pleasures at your right hand."
Psalm 16:11

REFLECTION QUESTIONS:
+ Share about a time in college when a friend was given an opportunity that you would've wanted. How did this affect the way you saw your circumstances?

+ Emily shares that "no number of friends was going to satisfy [her] deep longing for connection and intimacy with Jesus." Where do you run for immediate satisfaction? Have you let this take the place of intimacy with Jesus? Why?

DAY 2

We arrive at college expecting to find the friends God has always had for us, but often we feel extremely discouraged when those friends aren't revealed right away. When our hearts don't feel that instant connection, our desire to find genuine friendship only increases.

Have you ever experienced that yearning for connection in your loneliness? If not, maybe think about any instances when you felt isolated, or a time when you were surrounded by opportunities to fit in but didn't feel like you belonged.

It is often in those times of loneliness, with no weekend plans to distract us, that we finally open up the Word and seek authentic fullness. We have the choice either to seek people and worldly pleasures and receive temporary fulfillment, or to seek God's Word and receive growth, comfort, and true fulfillment.

The king of the universe wants to lean into you. As soon as we start diligently and intentionally seeking time with Him, we will find the never-ending love of God's heart and extended hand. When we intentionally stop making our community our Christ and instead dig into Scripture and prayer, we will find one impossibly loyal, wonderfully true, beautifully awesome friend in Jesus.

KEY VERSES:
"The Lord will guide you always; he will satisfy your needs in a sun-scorched land and will strengthen your frame. You will be like a well-watered garden, like a spring whose waters never fail."
Isaiah 58:11

REFLECTION QUESTIONS:
+ Have you been relying on your friends to be your source of fulfillment in college? How do you need to better balance your communion with Jesus versus time spent in community?

DAY 3

Even in our human imperfection, we know that earthly sources of satisfaction will always fail us and the only one who can be our everlasting source of life is Jesus. Although we know that our Lord loves us unconditionally and wants to fill us up, something in our hearts still puts that relationship with Him to the side and puts every other relationship first. How often do you tend to prefer wasting time with other people rather than committing to alone time with Jesus? Do you ever let your mind wander about what other people are doing or check social media during that quiet time? Do you ever wonder why our hearts have so much trouble just simply being still and resting in a quiet presence?

The enemy wants us to believe that spending quiet alone time resting in the Lord's presence is lazy or a waste of time. But what you have to remember is that when you let the living water of Christ pour into your soul, He supernaturally blesses you with more time and energy throughout your day. Don't run the worldly race. Don't take your available time with Jesus for granted. Remember who your Father is, and let Him fill your heart regardless of your schedule.

KEY VERSES:
"But whoever drinks the water I give them will never thirst. Indeed, the water I give them will become in them a spring of water welling up to eternal life."
John 4:14

"Come to me, all you who are weary and burdened, and I will give you rest. Take my yoke upon you and learn from me, for I am gentle and humble in heart, and you will find rest for your souls."
Matthew 11:28-29

REFLECTION QUESTIONS:
+ A lot of us know that God loves us, but that's different from feeling it deeply in our souls. In what ways are you lacking intimacy in your walk with the Lord? Have you been rushing a relationship or time with Him recently? How might you need to change your quiet time so that it feels less like a chore?

DAY 4

When God provides us with a sense of community, in His timing, we must keep in mind that what is making us feel full in time with community is not the actual community gatherings, it is Jesus.

How do we make spending fulfilling time with God a part of our everyday lives? In a world that tells us to chase after a full schedule, a perfect Instagram, and fun relationships to fill our hearts, is this even a practical goal? The answer to that depends on your willingness to surrender to Christ.

When we make the daily choice to sacrifice fifteen minutes of sleep to read our Bibles, the choice to pray instead of complaining, or discipline ourselves to meditate on a verse each day, we are able to see God's consistent work being done in our lives. He starts to soften our hearts, and bring us to our knees more than every once in a while. With hearts full from time with God, we start to experience awe and wonder in the little things in life. No more running the race of perfection. No more relying on other people to do what only God can do for you.

Starting today, let God take away your water fountain, and seek after His everlasting source of life and pure joy. He is all we have to satisfy our hearts' deepest desires, and that is all we need.

KEY VERSES:
"Better is one day in your court than a thousand elsewhere; I would rather be a doorkeeper in the house of my God than dwell in the tents of the wicked."
Psalm 84:10

REFLECTION QUESTIONS:
+ How do you need to leave more room for communion with Jesus? How could your life look different if you make the choice to go to Jesus first?

INDIA

LEE UNIVERSITY
ELEMENTARY EDUCATION
SOPHOMORE

Nearness In The Stillness

HEARING HIS WHISPERS IN THE QUIET MOMENTS

I remember the moment like it happened yesterday. I was driving down what is known as Stretch Road, and just as the name depicts, it's about a three-mile-long road that seems to drag on for an eternity. Camp-bound and full of excitement, I was blasting Hillsong music in anticipation—camp was just a few miles ahead. As I bounced along this pothole-filled, towering-tree-lined road, I prayed fervently for patience and strength. Little did I know that God would not only give me those gifts, but He would also present opportunities in which I could put them into practice.

As freshman year of college came to a close, I was filled with incredible excitement at the opportunity to return to this Christian camp that was very dear to my heart. Only this time, I was returning as a counselor rather than a camper. Freshman year had been both rewarding and challenging, and I had grown and changed quite a bit. As one of my dear friends once said, "Growing is not always fun or easy, but then again, I wouldn't want it any other way." I learned to trust God in new ways, as I was the oldest child in my family and therefore the first to leave home. The newness yielded so much beauty, and I was overjoyed at the opportunity to enter another new season as a camp counselor for the summer.

On the first day of camp, before the first batch of campers arrived, the leadership team had us spend some intentional time in prayer. They explained that they wanted each staffer to set apart time to go back to their individual cabin and simply be in prayer over everything that the Lord would do in and through each of us over the summer. When I got back to my cabin, the word "stillness" was resting in the back of my mind, so I searched in the concordance of my Bible for any verses related to this word. One specific verse caught my eye:

"Be still before the LORD, all mankind, because he has roused himself from his holy dwelling."
Zechariah 2:13

I almost overlooked it. In all honesty, I thought it would be one of those Old Testament verses that I couldn't truly apply to myself. But I looked closer and realized in that moment, on my knees on the hard wooden cabin floor, that Zechariah 2:13 would become my heart's verse for the summer. I am usually pretty quick to enter into a mindset of worry and anxiety in difficult situations, and I knew that I would have to be able to step away from that stress-filled worldview in order to truly serve my campers well that summer. I was only thinking of camp, but God would use this verse to shape and mold my heart well beyond that place and time.

First session was nothing short of life-changing. I was overwhelmed by the precious friendships I established with the other staffers, and the opportunities to pour into sweet girls for two weeks brought me indescribable joy. Witnessing one of my campers give her life to Jesus touched my heart so deeply, and I was ecstatic at the thought of getting to take part in this sort of Kingdom work all over again for the second session of camp! After all, I had the first session already under my belt, so I figured session two would be a breeze. In hindsight, I have realized that God was trying to show me something then which I'm only just now beginning to grasp: it's good to be expectant in our relationship with our Heavenly Father, but when we specify what we are expecting of God, we are limiting His capabilities in our minds. We are not leaving Him room to come in and do what He does best: move, work, and change.

I realized very quickly that my expectation for second session to be a duplication of the sweetness of that first session would not become reality. When my first camper for second session walked into Cabin 1, I was caught off guard by my first impression of her. From that first encounter, I knew it would not be the same experience as first session. She didn't even acknowledge my presence when I tried to greet her upon her arrival. I immediately recognized her from the photo attached to her background file that I had been given that morning—I knew that she had been abused at a young age, but the only information I had was that the first four years of her life were very traumatic. She was in a foster care system, and the foster parents stated in her paperwork that her past was no longer an emotional struggle for her. I, as well as the other staffers, quickly discovered that this was far from the truth.

Episode after episode occurred which revealed that this girl was facing major internal battles. I was constantly chasing after her as she ran away multiple times a day, she made threats toward the other seven-year-old girls, and her outbursts at night were terrifying. But the situation slowly got worse. Her physical aggression became a threat to not only me, but to my other campers. I had never felt so defeated, but I couldn't have been more grateful to have been surrounded by such caring and encouraging staffers. Other counselors whom I didn't even know came up to me and told me that they were praying for me. But the days were still long and hard. One time, my camper grabbed my glasses from my face, threw them across the room, shoved me to the floor, and slammed the door in my face. Another time, she had a violent night-episode and had to be carried out of the cabin by camp leadership. That night, she was told that if one more outburst occurred, she would have to be sent home.

"The LORD will fight for you; you need only to be still."
Exodus 14:14

As that night went on, after all the other campers were fast asleep, I sat in the hallway with fearful tears hitting the concrete floor. But I was surrounded by supportive, uplifting women of God who prayed over me and with me through those moments of anxiety and deep heart-pain. These were the moments in which I knew I had to rest in stillness, where I could feel His nearness. It's in these moments that we find comfort provided by the Holy Spirit's presence. Sitting in that stillness allows the Holy Spirit to move freely and work through us, but we have to intentionally choose it. I began to recognize the truth in Zechariah 2:13—God has roused Himself from His holy dwelling. He is not simply sitting on His throne observing all that is happening here on Earth. He is ever-present, fully and completely here with us. And that presence is a beautiful promise.

"The LORD replied, 'I will personally go with you, Moses, and I will give you rest—everything will be fine for you.'"
Exodus 33:14 NLT

The morning which followed that one late and restless night was a shock for me. My camper, treasured and cherished, looked at me and told me that she loved me. Rather than running away during worship, she sat quietly and actually took notes in her tiny sticker-covered journal. She didn't kick her fellow campers under the table at lunch. She didn't put up a fight when it was time for naps. She helped the other girls with their clean-up tasks for the day. My heart soared at the change that I was witnessing. But that afternoon, out of nowhere, she plummeted. And there I went again, chasing after her, pleading that she listen to me and obey. But the physical aggression came out once again, and it broke my heart to tell my supervisor that she had reached the point that our leadership had deemed to be the last straw. Disciplinary actions followed quickly, but having to hug her goodbye and watch her car fade into the distance was the worst moment of all. I poured my love into that precious child, but as she was leaving, I looked into her deep brown eyes and I could see the peace in her heart. I could see that she knew how much she was loved. That look made every hard moment, sleepless night, desperate prayer, downpour of tears, and plea for God's strength and stillness so worth it.

"This is what the Sovereign LORD, the Holy One of Israel, says: 'In repentance and rest is your salvation, in quietness and trust is your strength.'"
Isaiah 30:15

"He got up, rebuked the wind and said to the waves, 'Quiet! Be still!' Then the wind died down and it was completely calm."
Mark 4:39

Those two weeks of my life were hands-down the hardest two weeks of my entire life. I had never before felt so physically, emotionally, mentally, and spiritually drained all at the same time, but I wouldn't take back a single moment of that precious camper's time at camp. I learned that there will be moments in life when I literally cannot make it on my own strength—nor should I try. I learned what it takes to love like Jesus would love.

But most of all, God showed me what stillness looks like. In those moments when I was inches from giving up altogether, I saw the beauty in the silence, in the absence of motion, in the peace, and even in the solitude. I realized that sometimes we must allow ourselves to stop moving at such a chaotic pace, as though the fate of the world is on our shoulders.

This stillness is something that I am continuously working toward even in my daily college life. In the midst of the busy days, the hard days, and the long days, I am learning how this approach to quietness brings peace and builds intimacy with God. Whether I am struggling with schoolwork, friendships, or any other kind of trial that a college student might face, I have to stop myself and speak the same words over myself that Jesus spoke over the waves in Mark 4:39. Quiet. Be still. When we are still and seeking Him, He gives us what we need. For me it was strength that far surpassed any that I could muster up from within myself, peace that surpassed the whirlwind emotions of life around me, and patience that stretched beyond my own capabilities.

"Be still, and know that I am God; I will be exalted among the nations, I will be exalted in the earth."
Psalm 46:10

"The LORD said, 'Go out and stand on the mountain in the presence of the LORD, for the LORD is about to pass by.' Then a great and powerful wind tore the mountains apart and shattered the rocks before the LORD, but the LORD was not in the wind. After the wind there was an earthquake, but the LORD was not in the earthquake. After the earthquake came a fire, but the LORD was not in the fire. And after the fire came a gentle whisper."
1 Kings 19:11-12

As I was camp-bound and driving down Stretch Road, I had prayed for patience and strength. I'm now able to reflect on my time at camp and pinpoint the exact moments in which God provided those for me. But it took my willingness to step into the stillness to reach that point. Now I am here, in my sophomore year of college, still learning what God can do through my willingness to be still. I returned to the camp-bubble several weeks ago for a weekend girls' retreat, and I was once again reminded of how real and powerful God is. I went into the weekend feeling restless and worried because I had just found out that my living situation plans for junior year might fall through. As silly as it sounds, the worry captivated my thoughts and was at the forefront of my mind day and night. But as I drove toward camp, I stopped myself. I realized that just like at camp that past summer, I had to get out of that endless cycle of stressful thinking in order to truly serve God that weekend. So I once again spoke Jesus's words over myself: Quiet. Be still. I was able to step away from the worries that were consuming me, and didn't even think about my living situation once that weekend. When I turned my phone back on at the end of the technology-free retreat, would you believe what the first message on my phone read? My living situation was perfectly worked out—God handled everything. All I had to do was get out of His way and be still!

My favorite synonym for stillness is serenity. When I think of serenity, I think of a calm, peaceful, tranquil brook. The waters are moving gently and there's a sense of peace and safety—the kind of place where you could sit all day long without a worry in the world. When you sit in stillness, listening and watching, you can see harmony and tranquility. God is a lot like that brook, and I challenge you to sit in the stillness. Maybe that looks like solitude with a focused heart. Maybe it looks like simply stopping your mind from racing with worry. But it most certainly looks like a quiet and safe place.

Give God the chance to get a word in edgewise. Sit and listen. Listen to the waters moving, because even when it seems like they're motionless, I promise that they are stirring. It might just take that quiet solitude to hear the flowing current. Look for the harmony—this is who God is. He's sovereign, He's constant, He's faithful, and He is good. Sometimes it just takes those calm and quiet moments to hear His gentle whisper—that still small voice.

KEY VERSES:
Zechariah 2:13
Exodus 14:14
Exodus 33:14
Isaiah 30:15
Mark 4:39
Psalm 46:10
1 Kings 19:11-12

DISCUSSION QUESTIONS:
+ What emotions stir up in you as you think of being still, quiet, and alone? What makes it so difficult to sit alone with God?

+ What most often pulls you away from stillness with God? Is it stress, friends, work, relationships, etc.? Why are you placing more value on this than time with the Lord?

+ What part of your life needs to be surrendered to stillness? How might being still affect the situations in which you've been desperate for God's peace?

+ India shares, "I knew I had to rest in stillness, where I could feel His nearness." Have you been feeling distant from God because of a lack of quietness in your life? How would your relationship with Him grow if you became more dedicated to this area of your walk with the Lord?

+ Stillness doesn't mean that God is sitting still. When we are still, it actually allows God to move. In the midst of the busyness of college, have you misunderstood the discipline of stillness? What can you do to create a routine of this in your life?

DEVOTIONALS

CONTRIBUTOR: *Jana Rindler*

DAY 1

our names daily. Life constantly pulls us away from being still and distracts us from what our souls and hearts need most. Homework, parents, friendships, relationships, making sure you have a social life, and so much more. But there is always another voice calling our names among the chaos: the voice of God.

Am I the only one that has wished for God to send me a burning bush so I would know when He was speaking to me? More often than sending some obvious sign, He calls us to be still and listen for a whisper. When we are afraid of the unknown or feel anxious about what life has thrown at us, it's a normal reaction to run and cling to the anxious thoughts. But God calls us to something different. He calls us to seek His voice in the whisper and to be still. Being still is more than a physical posture, it's telling the restless waves in our heart and mind to quiet down—even to stop. It's surrendering control to God. Maybe it means keeping a key verse with you or listening to worship music as you walk through campus or as you do your homework. Maybe it means just saying His sweet yet powerful name out loud when you are anxious, asking him to still the restlessness and calm the storm.

KEY VERSES:
"After the earthquake came a fire, but the LORD was not in the fire. And after the fire came a gentle whisper."
1 Kings 19:12

"The LORD replied, 'I will personally go with you, Moses, and I will give you rest—everything will be fine for you.'"
Exodus 33:14 NLT

"He got up, rebuked the wind and said to the waves, 'Quiet! Be still!' Then the wind died down and it was completely calm."
Mark 4:39

REFLECTION QUESTIONS:
+ What emotions stir up in you as you think of being still, quiet, and alone? What makes it so difficult to sit alone with God?

+ What most often pulls you away from stillness with God? Is it stress, friends, work, relationships, etc.? Why are you placing more value on this than time with the Lord?

DAY 2

With the demands of life and college knocking on our door and trying to come in, it's so easy to get caught in the web of life. Sometimes we feel as if we can't go to God with these mundane things because they don't seem so important in comparison to world hunger and natural disaster. But even the things that we would think don't matter to God actually do matter to Him—because we matter to Him. It's amazing to think that both the little things and the big things of life, the boring and the exciting, are all important to our heavenly Father. And although He fights for you, He so badly wants to do this life with you.

God longs to be the one you run to when you feel anxious. He longs to whisper to the depths of your heart and give you exactly what you need. God doesn't want us to surrender just certain areas of our lives, He wants them all. He wants the stress, the worry, the anxiety, the bad thoughts, the good thoughts, the joy, the fun, etc. When we feel at our best, He wants to celebrate with us. When we feel we can't take another step, He wants to take us by the hand. There is nothing that our God can't handle. He is a victorious warrior and He is fighting on your behalf.

KEY VERSES:
"The LORD your God is with you, the Mighty Warrior who saves. He will take great delight in you; in His love He will no longer rebuke you, but will rejoice over you with singing."
Zephaniah 3:17

"The LORD will fight for you; you need only to be still."
Exodus 14:14

REFLECTION QUESTIONS:
+ What part of your life needs to be surrendered to stillness? How might being still affect the situations in which you've been desperate for God's peace?

If someone were to sit across from you at a little café and ask if you have been still lately, what would you say? This isn't about being still and reading a book or laying down and watching Netflix all night. Have you been still, hushed, motionless, quiet, free from distraction, and in His presence? There are plenty of things demanding our affection, time, and attention, pulling us away from our relationship with Jesus.

Being still is more than talking to God and expressing your heart, it's waiting for Him to express His heart to you. James 4:8 says that when we draw near to Him, He will draw near to us. That's the beauty of the stillness. That's the beauty of freeing ourselves from distractions to seek His presence.

In the stressful moments, run to Him. In the anxious moments, run to Him. In the exciting moments, run to Him. As we draw near to Him and learn to be still, He ignites and renews our zeal for Him. He molds our hearts to look like His and fixes the pieces that have been broken for so long. Amazingly, as much as we desire this closeness to God, He wants it even more.

KEY VERSES:
"Come near to God and he will come near to you."
James 4:8

"Be still, and know that I am God; I will be exalted among the nations, I will be exalted in the earth."
Psalm 46:10

REFLECTION QUESTIONS:
+ India shares, "I knew I had to rest in stillness, where I could feel His nearness." Have you been feeling distant from God because of a lack of quietness in your life? How would your relationship with Him grow if you became more dedicated to this area of your walk with the Lord?

DAY 4

Being still is not a suggestion, it's a command and God's desire for us. Being still is so much more than the physical act of stopping. It involves remembering who your God is, surrendering, and humbling ourselves before Him. It is choosing Him and His way.

When's the last time you read the story of Mary and Martha in the Gospel of Luke? It's infamous in church as the tale of two sisters who hosted Jesus in their home and responded to Him very differently. Martha was distracted by serving Jesus, while Mary simply sat at His feet. Martha got frustrated with her sister for not helping and even asked Jesus to command her to help. But Jesus told Martha that she was worried about many things, and that Mary chose the better way, sitting at the feet of Jesus listening and learning.

This is the same opportunity we receive day after day. So often we are Martha, too busy "serving" to realize that Jesus is simply calling us to surrender to stillness with Him. This art of surrender is a discipline we need to pursue every morning, afternoon, evening, and night.

Reflect on whether the choices you make lead you to stillness. Are you being led by your emotions or are you resting in Him? This isn't easy. It takes that little mustard seed of faith. Each of us has heard the call to give up something specific in order to pursue Him. Social media will still be there. Netflix can wait. Homework, as important as it is, can wait too. There is nothing worthy of sacrificing the precious time we could spend with Him. Growing a friendship with Jesus is priceless, sweet, and rejuvenating. Nothing can compare to time spent at His feet.

KEY VERSES:
"As Jesus and his disciples were on their way, he came to a village where a woman named Martha opened her home to him. She had a sister called Mary, who sat at the Lord's feet listening to what he said. But Martha was distracted by all the preparations that had to be made. She came to him and asked, 'Lord, don't you care that my sister has left me to do the work by myself? Tell her to help me!'
'Martha, Martha,' the Lord answered, 'you are worried and upset about many things, but few things are needed—or indeed only one. Mary has chosen what is better, and it will not be taken away from her.'"
Luke 10:38-42

"This is what the Sovereign LORD, the Holy One of Israel, says: 'In repentance and rest is your salvation, in quietness and trust is your strength.'"
Isaiah 30:15

REFLECTION QUESTIONS:
+ Stillness doesn't mean that God is sitting still. When we are still, it actually allows God to move. In the midst of the busyness of college, have you misunderstood the discipline of stillness? What can you do to create a routine of this in your life?

KATIE

BELMONT UNIVERSITY
EDUCATION & COMMUNICATIONS
FRESHMAN

Learning To Forgive

SHOWING GRACE AND LOVE TO THOSE WHO HURT US

It all started with the most exciting event of 2018 in Nashville, Tennessee: the solar eclipse. I sat with a bunch of people I had met through orientation and Welcome Week and together we witnessed the magic. We got along great, had instant chemistry, and I seriously had the best day. Naturally, I thought I'd found my forever friends. The friends who would study with me in the library, who would accompany me on late-night milkshake runs, and who would be in my graduation pics at the end of senior year. In my mind, I had finally found my people!

To say that I had high expectations about the friends I'd meet in college was an understatement. I just knew that I'd finally meet my best friends and have the type of friend group depicted in movies. I couldn't wait to fully get to know and love a group of people and to have them fully know and love me in return.

For the first five months of college, we hung out together constantly. We went to concerts, had movie nights, celebrated birthdays, played on the same intramural teams, went out to dinner, and explored Nashville together. We all had so much fun and truly loved being around each other. But slowly, as each of us became more comfortable within the group, some of the once lighthearted jokes that were meant to make everyone laugh turned into jabs that felt cruel and harsh. One person in particular started to make awful jokes that were directed toward specific people. Feelings were hurt, and what was intended as "joking around" became inappropriate and offensive.

"Therefore, my dear brothers and sisters, stand firm. Let nothing move you. Always give yourselves fully to the work of the Lord, because you know that your labor in the Lord is not in vain."
1 Corinthians 15:58

I stand up for the people I love and for what I believe, so I would call this person out each time they said something offensive. Unfortunately,

I was usually the only person to speak out. The conflict led that person to become, let's just say, not my biggest fan. Because of this, I slowly but surely felt less and less connected to the group.

Despite this, I came back to campus after winter break ready to dive into the second semester of my freshman year with all of my newfound friends—just to find that the tension had escalated. The semester began with my head spinning and my heart hurting. The day we all returned to school was my birthday, and not a single one of them spoke to me or wished me a happy birthday. I invited all of them to celebrate that day and didn't even receive a response. And even though that day was so hard for me, I ignored all of the unkindness and stayed with this group, scared of losing the friendships in it that I did value.

We've all been there before. At the beginning of college, you're thrown into a new environment where you maybe know a handful of people, if any at all. It's natural to want to make new friends and have people to hang out with. And since everyone is feeling that way, we try and create a space to fit into by forcing friendships that may be unhealthy. I know in hindsight that the friendships I had within that group definitely weren't meant to be, but at the time I kept trying to make them work because I desired a sense of security.

Soon, the group chat we used to make plans was totally inactive, but I knew they were still hanging out without me. Eventually I found out that they had created a new group chat—and it obviously didn't include me. Upon discovering I was being excluded, I blamed myself for those friends treating me poorly and began to question my worth.

I had considered some of those people my closest friends. How could they just kick me out like that? Why wasn't I important enough to defend? Did they ever care about me at all? How could God have let this happen to me? Did He not want me to have friends in college? These questions swam around in my mind for weeks and brought up doubt, shame, loneliness, and insecurity. For weeks, I avoided all of my other friends as well and began to shut people out in an effort to hide the hurt I was feeling.

I was so angry with these "friends" and how they had treated me that I carried the anger around for weeks. The bitterness showed up in everything that I did, everywhere I went. Every single day I felt consumed by frustration and hurt toward this group of people. I prayed to the Lord and asked Him to help me move on. Although I wanted so badly to forget it all, I wasn't willing to forgive. The grudge I was holding was tearing me apart no matter how long or hard I prayed to Jesus for help. I finally realized that in order to move on, I had to let go of my anger and search in my heart for the forgiveness I needed to extend to this group. I had to be real with myself about the expectations I had placed on these people and how it had played a part in the hurt I was feeling so deeply.

The hurt I felt and subsequent avoidance efforts were affecting so many other aspects of my life that I decided I needed additional guidance. I ended up going to counseling at my school to seek some advice regarding healthy friendships and what it might look like to move on. My counselor told me something that deeply resonated with me and prompted my journey of healing. He said, "Holding a grudge and carrying the anger you're feeling is like drinking poison and hoping for the person you're angry with to feel it."

"Get rid of all bitterness, rage and anger, brawling and slander, along with every form of malice. Be kind and compassionate to one another, forgiving each other, just as in Christ God forgave you."
Ephesians 4:31-32

One of the biggest struggles I faced during this time of giving the Lord control over my heart and life was learning to forgive. Honestly, it took a really long time for me to find the strength in myself to forgive those people for hurting me so deeply. I had always equated forgiveness with telling someone that they didn't do anything wrong, so it was hard for me to forgive those friends when I felt they had clearly done me wrong. Throughout my healing process I gradually realized that forgiving them didn't mean that what they did was okay, it meant that I was ready to move on from the pain. In order to release the heavy weight of the anger, resentment, and hurt that still burdened my heart, and to shape my own life on my terms without any unnecessary worries holding me down—I finally forgave them.

"[Love] keeps no record of wrongs."
1 Corinthians 13:5

I made the choice to forgive that group of friends after many weeks of struggling to make sense of my emotions, and it was one of the most freeing decisions I've ever made. Forgiveness is a commitment to show love and mercy rather than hold a grudge that truly only hurts you. I didn't forgive them because I was weak or gave into their apologies. I didn't even receive or expect to receive an apology from most of those friends. I forgave them because I finally stopped looking to those people to define or bring me worth and value, and instead looked to the Lord.

Even though forgiveness might feel like giving up or giving in, truly it's the grace of God working in us. We are constantly forgiven for our sins, and sometimes we don't even apologize for them. God recognizes our mistakes and graciously forgives us, showing us His unconditional love and grace. Because of His unending strength and constant forgiveness, I am able to do the same in showing grace and forgiveness to the friends who hurt me.

"Even if they sin against you seven times in a day and seven times come back to you saying 'I repent,' you must forgive them."
Luke 17:4

I still haven't mastered forgiveness or learned how to perfect my relationship with the Lord, but I now make sure that I set aside time each day to talk with the Lord and thank Him for everything He does for me. Praying to and confiding in Jesus was my strength when I felt so alone and weak—knowing that He hears my prayers, calms my anxiety, and speaks truth into my insecurities while also reminding me how loved I am.

"For God has said, 'I will never fail you. I will never abandon you.'"
Hebrews 13:5 NLT

One Sunday at church, our worship team sang the song "Do It Again" by Elevation Worship. The lyrics say, "I'm still in your hands, this is my confidence: You've never failed me yet." These words echoed in my heart, and I found myself sitting down during worship for the first time in months. I felt so guilty for spending so much time mourning the loss of friendships with people who didn't really care about me, when the Lord loves me more in one moment than anyone on this earth could in a lifetime.

I grow more and more confident in the Lord's faithfulness and love for me each day. He has helped me to recognize my worth and value as His child, and that I deserve love and true friendship rather than the types of friendships I had been pouring myself into. I thank God for protecting me by ending relationships I thought I really wanted, an outcome I didn't know I needed at the time. Instead He gave me friends who, I have grown to realize, love me deeper and more boldly than I ever knew I needed. The Lord's plan and purpose for my life is so much greater than anything I could ever plan for myself or even imagine. If the hurt I experienced is going to help shape me into the woman God intends for me to be, then I need to trust in that.

"For we live by faith, not by sight."
2 Corinthians 5:7

My dependence on my friends to make me feel worthy and loved prevented me from pursuing a relationship with the Lord. I learned that even if we don't understand the purpose of the season we're walking through, it's important to wait patiently and trust in the Lord's love for us and His plan. Holding onto anger and resentment only hurts you. Once you forgive someone for hurting you, the weight of those emotions you've been carrying around can be lifted, and the freedom found in forgiving others will amaze you.

"For you created my inmost being; you knit me together in my mother's womb. I praise you because I am fearfully and wonderfully made; your works are wonderful, I know that full well." Psalm 139:13-14
Even though I did forgive those friends who hurt me, I was careful to not let my forgiveness become foolishness. I'm cordial with most of them when we run into each other on campus, and of course it stings a little bit, but that hurt doesn't control me in the way that it used to. Now, I put time and effort into other friendships that I hadn't been able to before because I was too busy trying to force relationships that weren't meant to be. These friendships found me at the most unexpected times and happened naturally. Even though it felt like a long time before I had friends who truly loved and cared about me, the value of their friendship was worth the wait.

God brings certain people into our lives to strengthen who we are by teaching us about His own character. Even though these relationships seemed terrible and toxic, I'm grateful for the way God turned my negative circumstances into a positive lesson about forgiveness, further molding my heart into His. God uses all things for His glory. Even in the most difficult trials, He will reveal how He is making all things new—you simply have to ask Him.

Have you held back forgiveness from somebody specific? How can you show them the grace and forgiveness that the Lord shows us daily? Be gentle with yourself and remember that this struggle won't go away instantly. The first and most difficult step is becoming self-aware enough to admit you're not ready to forgive that person. I would also encourage you to figure out whether you need to forgive them in person or not. In my case, I kept it to myself because it was only hurting me. If you need to tell someone you forgive them in order to receive freedom, then send that text, make that call, or write that email. You will feel so much better when you do. Even though my journey didn't progress as quickly as I hoped, the benefits of releasing my bitterness were immediately noticeable. After finally letting go of my hurt and anger, and feeling more content with myself, my days were happier and brighter. Replacing your grudge with actively surrendering to the Lord's will—pursuing His forgiveness, grace, and love—will bring you abundant life and relentless joy.

KEY VERSES:
1 Corinthians 15:58
Ephesians 4:31-32
1 Corinthians 13:5
Luke 17:4
Hebrews 13:5
2 Corinthians 5:7
Psalm 139:13-14

DISCUSSION QUESTIONS:
+ What expectations do you carry about friendship? How do these expectations play into the way you respond to or treat your relationships?

+ Has there been a time when you were let down or hurt by a friend? How did this affect the way you view yourself? If you are being honest with yourself, is this hard for you to overcome?

+ What slivers of disappointment or anger do you hold in your heart? Why haven't you acknowledged or dealt with these feelings? What could be a first step toward healing?

+ Most often, healing happens when you're able to recognize your own faults in the relationship. In what ways have you been carrying pride in the process of forgiving? Even when it doesn't feel like your fault, how can you take ownership in the forgiveness process?

+ Katie explains that, "Forgiveness is a commitment to show love and mercy rather than hold a grudge that truly only hurts you." How do you need to regularly show God's love and mercy to your friends? How would this change the trajectory of your friendships?

DEVOTIONALS

CONTRIBUTOR: *MacKenzie Wilson*

DAY 1

Like Katie, we probably all arrived at college thinking that we'd find our lifelong best friends during the first semester. Maybe they would be our suitemates, or the group of girls that lived down the hall. Maybe the study group from our freshman seminar class, or that fun group of people from our intramural flag football team.

Often times in college, you click with a group of people and then dive headfirst into relationships because you're looking for a security blanket in the midst of a huge and daunting transition. Sometimes this gets you stuck in friendships that aren't the most life-giving. And even when you come to realize it's time to detach, it can be difficult to break away because of the fear that you'll be left with no friends at all. Sometimes it leaves you relying on new friends and expecting more out of them than you perhaps should.

Think back to the expectations you had for friendships coming into college. Do you think these expectations have played a part in the way your friendships have turned out? Take a step back this week to examine your friendships and ask yourself whether God is at the center of those relationships. Where have your expectations gotten in the way? How can you trust the Lord to guide your friendships in the future?

The first step to entering into healthy friendships is being able to come clean about the reality of their current state. Maybe you're holding your friends to unrealistic expectations that they'll never meet, or maybe you're only maintaining certain relationships because you're afraid to be alone at college. Be honest with yourself and let God be a part of what you do with them moving forward. Invite Him to transform, renew, and re-establish your friendships at school.

KEY VERSES:

"Know also that wisdom is like honey for you: If you find it, there is a future hope for you, and your hope will not be cut off."not be a servant of Christ."

Proverbs 24:14

REFLECTION QUESTIONS:

+ What expectations do you carry about friendship? How do these expectations play into the way you respond to or treat your relationships?

Friendship wounds cause some of the deepest pain we experience. Everyone wants to feel accepted, known, loved, and pursued by the people around them. But in reality, sometimes the people we love hurt us, and instead we feel rejected, unseen, forgotten about, and left out in the cold. This rejection leaves us questioning our value and worth and even doubting God's intentions for good things in our lives. These moments can plant seeds of bitterness and resentment in our hearts that grow unruly, like weeds in a garden, without us even noticing. Are there past hurts from friendships in your life that you haven't fully acknowledged?

Yesterday we talked about recognizing expectations and the current state of your friendships, but it's also important to understand how your past is having an impact on your present. We have to uncover and address the silvers of disappointment or anger that we carry in the deep places of our hearts. We must bring them to the surface so that we can gather them up and carry them to the feet of Jesus. He's the only one who can rewrite the pain we might still be feeling from past disappointments. He is the only one able to set us free from the chains we've been wearing. The Lord desires to free us so He can send us back out, fully loved and fully known, ready to pass on His grace to the people around us.

KEY VERSES:
"The LORD is close to the brokenhearted and saves those who are crushed in spirit."
Psalm 34:18

REFLECTION QUESTIONS:
+ Has there been a time when you were let down or hurt by a friend? How did this affect the way you view yourself? If you are being honest with yourself, is this hard for you to overcome?

+ What slivers of disappointment or anger do you hold in your heart? Why haven't you acknowledged or dealt with these feelings? What could be a first step toward healing?

DAY 3

"Holding a grudge and carrying the anger you're feeling is like drinking poison and hoping for the person you're angry with to feel it."

How often does the mentality from the statement above slip into our healing and forgiveness process? We spend so much time concerned with the other person, hoping that they will realize and make amends for the hurt they put us through, that we slip into a dangerous cycle of resentment. We start to drink the poison of bitterness.

But instead of obsessing over every specific way the other person hurt us, God calls us to shine a spotlight on our own hearts to see the ways that we might have played a part in the problem. There is so much freedom and forgiveness to be found when we recognize that all the blame isn't on the other person's shoulders, even when you truly feel like they were the one in the wrong. Maybe your expectations of them were too high, maybe you didn't go a great job communicating your hurt, or maybe you've simply been blind to the ways that you hurt them too. Ask God to help you search your heart this week and to lead you in taking ownership in the forgiveness process.

KEY VERSES:
"Search me, God, and know my heart; test me and know my anxious thoughts. See if there is any offensive way in me, and lead me in the way everlasting."
Psalm 139:23-34

REFLECTION QUESTIONS:
+ Most often, healing happens when you're able to recognize your own faults in the relationship. In what ways have you been carrying pride in the process of forgiving? Even when it doesn't feel like your fault, how can you take ownership in the forgiveness process?

DAY 4

We get the best versions of people when we create an environment for them to feel fully seen, known, and loved for exactly who they are. We get the versions of people who will speak life into us, who will pick us up when we fall, and who will challenge and encourage us to be the best versions of ourselves.

When we are closed off, guarded, and always on the defense, then we will get friends who will treat us the same way in return. Be the type of friend who creates an environment for other people to take down their defenses. Your friendships change for the better when you focus on others rather than always being consumed by your own thoughts, feelings, and emotions. Cultivating a servant heart within all your relationships will attract people who are sold out for Jesus and looking to invest in healthy Christ-centered friendships.

Always be the first to extend grace within your friendships. Be the first to show up when your people need you. Go the extra mile and care for people before they've proven themselves "worthy" of your time and attention. Love like Jesus would, and watch as He brings the people into your life who will love you in the same way.

KEY VERSES:
"Get rid of all bitterness, rage and anger, brawling and slander, along with every form of malice. Be kind and compassionate to one another, forgiving each other, just as in Christ God forgave you."
Ephesians 4:31-32

"[Love] keeps no record of wrongs."
1 Corinthians 13:5

REFLECTION QUESTIONS:
+ Katie explains that, "Forgiveness is a commitment to show love and mercy rather than hold a grudge that truly only hurts you." How do you need to regularly show God's love and mercy to your friends? How would this change the trajectory of your friendships?

ANGEL

LIBERTY UNIVERSITY
ENTREPRENEURSHIP
JUNIOR

The Pursuit of Perfection

TAKING OUR EYES OFF OUR INSECURITIES AND LOOKING TO GOD

This is for the girl who looks in the mirror and hates what she sees. This is for the girl who is exhausted down to her very bones, who is tired from chasing an ever-evolving standard of beauty, desperately trying to conform to an image that isn't even real. The girl who is so strung out on people-pleasing and comparison that she is missing the life that is right in front of her.

That girl was me.

I was always chasing what I could never attain, searching for an image that didn't even exist. I chased it at a size 6, and I chased it at a size 2; it didn't matter. For too long, I was held prisoner to perfectionism, people-pleasing, comparison, and insecurity. They stole my freedom, robbed me of my confidence, and told me to put my gifts on a shelf, convincing me that those gifts were laughable, unusable. I've missed so much of my precious human life trying to force things into a tiny compartment of "perfect", trying to prove to the world I was enough. I know what it's like to live as a slave for so long that it becomes part of the fabric of your soul. But I am also here to tell you there is a freedom offered to you that is far beyond what you ever imagined. The bad news is that you can't win this battle accidentally or by hiding in that compartment of fear—but the good news is that it's already been won.

Let me take you back to the girl who was sleepwalking through life, the girl who pursued the things of the world instead of the one who created the world. Everyday life started by waking up in the morning already consumed by thoughts of losing weight. I spent my high school days focusing on all the wrong things, finding my identity in all the wrong places. My worth and emotions were on a constant roller coaster ride because I sought my worth in the approval of people, especially boys. I had to have eyes on me at all times. When I walked by, I wanted people to notice.

I lived in a state of relentless, paralyzing comparison. Her body. Her personality. Her grades. My friendships lacked depth; the comparison game would add layer upon layer to the thick walls surrounding my heart as it kept me perpetually measuring how I ranked against everyone else. My relationship with food and exercise began to plummet too. There is a fine line between dedication and obsession, and I had no regard for it. I would wake up at 5:00 a.m. every day and work out because I told myself I had to be thin. After sports practice, I would run for miles because I thought I had to, definitely not because I wanted to. I would sacrifice just about anything to make sure I got my workout in, and missing a session would send me into an emotional spiral. When it came to food, I had slowly become meticulous about every single calorie I ate. I refused to eat at restaurants because it made me feel out of control. For months, any time I was invited to a meal with my family or friends, I would sit there and watch them eat. My obsession with appearance was destroying my relationships in ways I didn't even see or fully understand. The sad part about it all is that the leaner I was, the unhappier I became. The pursuit of perfection was decimating me. I was consumed, I was miserable, and I wasn't living.

I look back at the girl I was, and I can't recognize her. Let me tell you what real, tangible freedom looks like in the daily mundane college student life. Last semester, there was a time I was really struggling with the way I looked, and the weight of comparison was heavy. This season was full of prayer and surrender, but also frustration and disappointment. Much of what I felt like I had won victory over came creeping up even stronger and uglier than before.

Oftentimes God teaches lessons over a long span of time, but sometimes He reveals something that just makes everything click in a single moment. As someone who only felt confident walking into the gym with a full face of makeup and a cute sporty outfit, I dreaded going there dressed in my baggy t-shirt and hat that covered my third-day-unwashed hair. But instead of feeling insecure and small, God spoke to me in a way that I'd never heard or listened to before. He told me that I didn't need to focus on the boys looking at other girls in the gym as I so often did. As temptation to compare myself arose He whispered, Angel, I didn't create you to be like her. I created you to be you.

For the first time, I felt free from the lies constantly clouding my mind. In hindsight, this was the starting point of God teaching me to truly believe in my heart the things I had known in my head. He showed me what confidence in Him looks like—not grounded in fleeting feelings of superiority to others, but rather a confidence of security grounded in knowing that I didn't need to compare myself to anyone at all. God told me that I didn't need to crave being seen by others, because He already sees me and knows me.

Whatever you're struggling with, God is offering freedom—although it may not always arrive in a grand breakthrough. If you are desperately praying over something that you believe has a hold on you, I want you to know that God has already overcome it. I remember getting so angry at myself for struggling with the same things over and over again. Countless nights I felt defeated because I couldn't seem to give over the thing that held me from Jesus; as much as I wanted to, I just didn't know how. In these seasons, God taught me that the process of freedom is in the journey rather than the destination. All I needed to do was go to Him.

For most of my life, I simply dealt with so many side effects of poor body image rather than looking deeper to the primary source: pride. What a cold, scary word. There's no grace or love in pride. And how could somebody so insecure be so prideful?

God has shown me that the root of my insecurity wasn't that I was thinking too much or too little of myself, it was that I was thinking of myself too much. He has shown me that I will never feel better about myself by becoming more consumed with myself. I now see my self-worship and obsession. Pride had been driving me all along, whispering lies, perpetually pushing me in the opposite direction of the fulfillment it promised.

In our American culture, the media preaches that the way to cure harmful body image is by learning to love our bodies. They tell us that confidence is as easy as loving our eyes, even if we don't love our thighs. But freedom is not found in loving our imperfections. It's found in loving Jesus. Did you know Satan was beautiful? Though Satan possessed a high place in heaven, power, musical ability, and beauty, he chose that those were not enough. Instead, he rebelled. God said:

"Your heart became proud on account of your beauty, and you corrupted your wisdom because of your splendor. So I threw you to the earth; I made a spectacle of you before kings."
Ezekiel 28:17

Satan was beautiful, but his pride in his beauty led to his ultimate destruction. Just as it has been proven time after time in my own life, any form of pride paves the path to destruction. Satan wanted to be like God, then God created man in His own image. Satan hates man because we were made in God's likeness and reflect the image of the King he could never be.

I'm no expert at this, and sometimes I need these words most of all, but the remedy for freedom no longer remains unanswered for me. The antidote to my pride was a big dose of humility. Freedom is found in the place where I lose my life for the sake of something greater. God has shown me that the more willing I am to get outside of my own life, the more I will find where true, full life abounds.

"What is more, I consider everything a loss because of the surpassing worth of knowing Christ Jesus my Lord, for whose sake I have lost all things. I consider them garbage, that I may gain Christ."
Philippians 3:8

He has transformed what motivates me. He has helped me stop using people as my mirror and to instead start seeing myself as He alone sees me. I now realize I have a choice; we all have a choice. We can stand up against the world and decide that the lie it's selling is not worth buying— the price is too high. We can rest in the truth that life is not found there.

These words might sound pretty and nice, but what about the days when humility seems unattainable and pride is entangling? How can we practically instruct our hearts to walk in such truth every day? I recently came across a story in the gospels in which Jesus walks on water. I thought I knew this story well because I'd been hearing it taught since I was a child in Sunday school, but the Holy Spirit whispered truth to me in a whole new manner.

"'Come,' he said. Then Peter got down out of the boat, walked on the water and came toward Jesus. But when he saw the wind, he was afraid and, beginning to sink, cried out, 'Lord, save me!'"
Matthew 14:29-30

It wasn't until Peter saw the wind that he was afraid and began to sink. When Peter took his eyes off Jesus and focused on the world around him, he became overwhelmed by his circumstances and doubt. When we take our eyes off Jesus, we are left with ourselves. But the beautiful part is the story doesn't end there. As Peter began to sink he cried, "Lord, save me!" and Jesus immediately reached out His hand. He is always reaching out His hand, waiting to save you. As I continue to step out of the boat, into the daily storms of this world, I'm learning to fix my gaze on the one who created my soul and has called me to Him. The one with love in His eyes, the only one who will rescue me despite my flaws. The reality is, we are all following something. Why don't we focus on the one who goes before us instead of all that surrounds us? I know that when I stare at the face of Christ long enough, I am able to see myself more clearly, and I believe that can be true for you too.

"Let your eyes look straight ahead; fix your gaze directly before you."
Proverbs 4:25

Comparison wasn't meant to be such a negative notion. We were created to want to compare ourselves—not to other people, but to the Holy Spirit in us. When we compare ourselves to the Holy Spirit, we can see identify where we need to work on patience or peace, kindness or humility. Comparing ourselves to other people through the Holy Spirit also becomes positive, as we can identify, call out, and encourage the growth of fruit in other people instead of being jealous. Why don't we seek first the face of Jesus every morning before we look to Instagram or the mirror? I promise you, when we look to Jesus first, His presence changes everything. In the midst of my insatiable quest for beauty, I didn't realize all that it was really stealing from me; all the ways it affected my relationship with God, myself, and my purpose. This cycle is the tragedy that keeps us chasing the wrong things. I spent most of my life being fixated on what I didn't have or what I thought I should be. I spent so much time disliking what I had been given that I forgot why I had it in the first place.

I spent my life giving it away to something or to someone, until God reminded me that I was created to give myself to purpose—His true and perfect purpose. I don't want to look back at my life in twenty years and realize the best thing about myself was that I had shiny hair and a flat stomach. I've learned that our worth can't always be rooted in what we feel, it has to be rooted in what we know about ourselves as God's children.

When I immersed myself in serving others with my passions and gifts, the weight of my appearance wasn't the focus anymore. I found value in empowering others, therefore empowering myself, as I became more selfless. We were handcrafted with love by the God of the universe. He planted a set of dreams and gifts inside each of us. Entrusted to you are things of great value, entrusted to you and only you. Everything you were made to be is not an accident.

"My frame was not hidden from you when I was made in the secret place, when I was woven together in the depths of the earth. Your eyes saw my unformed body; all the days ordained for me were written in your book before one of them came to be."
Psalm 139:15-16

What are you good at? What are you crazy about? When do you feel most alive, even if nobody else thinks so? Where's the need? You were created to find the place where your passions meet the world's deepest needs. You were created to fill gaps. To those of you who think your gifts are of little value, let me encourage you that it's not about what you have but whose you are. Satan hates us because we are children of God and have access to everything Jesus had. I have found that what the enemy cannot take from us, he will try to convince us to give away. He will whisper lies that these gifts have no value. The reason you have breath in your lungs is not to chase the ever-changing definition of beauty but to help display things as our Creator intended them to be, to make Him known. Where in your life have you taken your eyes off Jesus and instead focused on the issues of this world? My appearance had me distracted from my purpose for far too long. Now instead of insecurity and comparison, He has flooded my life with purpose and compassion. He is my strength in weakness. I know that nothing is without purpose, and nothing is out of His plan. I know that everything given to me is specific to the destiny He ordained before time began.

Let's stop chasing the wrong things; He made us to change the world.

KEY VERSES:
Ezekiel 28:17
Philippians 3:8
Matthew 14:29-30
Proverbs 4:25
Psalm 139:15-16

DISCUSSION QUESTIONS:
+ Have you been consumed by thoughts about the way you look? What has caused you to become a prisoner to perfectionism?

+ What are the side effects of your need to feel beautiful? What is the deeper issue that you haven't dealt with yet?

+ The world often convinces us that the answer to our insecurities is learning to love our bodies more, but true freedom is found in learning to love God more. Have your insecurities magnified your own image rather than God? How would shifting your gaze from yourself to God reshape the way that you view yourself?

+ Angel shares, "Freedom is found in the place where I lose my life for the sake of something greater. God has shown me that the more willing I am to get outside of my own life, the more I will find where true, full life abounds." What have you been missing because of the time you've spent trying to perfect your image? How can you stop obsessing over trying to perfect your own image and start focusing on reflecting the image of God?

+ Is there anything in your life that you need to release because it is creating a cycle of comparison? How can you practically go to Jesus first, rather than social media or the mirror?

DEVOTIONALS

CONTRIBUTOR: *MacKenzie Wilson*

DAY 1

Have you ever obsessed over the way you looked? Maybe it was that morning you felt like crap because of the massive amount of ice cream, flaming hot Cheetos, and popcorn you ate the night before. Maybe it's the day you walked into a party and felt like everyone else had just stepped straight off the set of the Kardashians while you looked like you had just rolled out of bed. Maybe it's the week you dieted and worked out like crazy to fit into that dress and the zipper still wouldn't zip. We've all had those days where obsessive thoughts about the way we looked clouded our mind.

There's this common desire in all of us to feel beautiful, desired, and loved. This desire will rear its ugly head in our lives in a lot of different ways. It might show up through dieting and excessive working out, wearing copious amounts of makeup, or looking to relationships for affirmation. Regardless of the form it takes, there's usually a deeper issue going on beneath the side effects of our need to feel beautiful. Is it possible you're struggling with perfection and obsessing over the way you look because you're not letting the Lord's voice be the loudest in your life? Take some time today to identify the voices in your life that are speaking louder than His and recognize how they are coming to the surface in your thoughts and actions. The first step to overcoming them is recognizing them and then taking them to the feet of Jesus. He's the only one who can silence the other voices. Give Him the time and space to speak truth over who you are and how He sees you.

KEY VERSES:
"I praise you because I am fearfully and wonderfully made; your works are wonderful, I know that full well."
Psalm 139:14

REFLECTION QUESTIONS:
+ Have you been consumed by thoughts about the way you look? What has caused you to become a prisoner to perfectionism?

+ What are the side effects of your need to feel beautiful? What is the deeper issue that you haven't dealt with yet?

DAY 2

There are a million "quick fixes" out there to help you overcome insecurities and love your body more. All you have to do is scroll through Instagram for all of five minutes and you'll have some fitness blogger sharing about a new workout to try in the gym. Give Pinterest ten minutes of your day and you'll discover a new paleo, gluten-free, calorie-less donut recipe that will help you finally reach your goal weight. If it's not a diet or exercise program, then it's a mantra which, if you chant five times a day in the mirror, will make you suddenly love everything about yourself. The truth of the matter is that these "solutions" rarely work, and if by some fluke they do, several weeks later you'll find yourself right back to where you started—obsessing over the way you look.

The answer to truly overcoming our insecurities doesn't lie in learning to love our bodies more. The true answer lies in learning to love God more. The more that we love God and understand His heart for us and the purpose He has in mind for our lives, the less we will fixate on the small and minute parts of our lives. Suddenly instead of obsessing over the things we hate about our appearance, we start to notice the amazing parts of us that God can use for His good and for His glory. Instead of always seeing what we think we lack, we begin to see the abundance of blessings God has given to us. When we learn to love God more, our perspective changes and all of life changes with it. Getting to know God and counting everything else as loss allows us to gain our life back and see the beauty that will come from it.

KEY VERSES:
"What is more, I consider everything a loss because of the surpassing worth of knowing Christ Jesus my Lord, for whose sake I have lost all things. I consider them garbage, that I may gain Christ."
Philippians 3:8

REFLECTION QUESTIONS:
+ The world often convinces us that the answer to our insecurities is learning to love our bodies more, but true freedom is found in learning to love God more. Have your insecurities magnified your own image rather than God? How would shifting your gaze from yourself to God reshape the way that you view yourself?

DAY 3

Think back on your last week and take note of all the time you spent trying to perfect your image. How much time did you spend trying to look a certain way so someone would finally notice you? How much time did you spend doing something to impress someone? How much time did you spend scrolling through Instagram comparing your life to strangers on the internet?

We're all bound and chained to this cycle of comparison and obsessing over how others see us. We love this quote from Angel that says, "Freedom is found in the place where I lose my life for the sake of something greater. God has shown me that the more willing I am to get outside of my own life, the more I will find where true, full life abounds."

What have you been missing out on because you've been enslaved to this cycle of perfection and comparison? Spend some time thinking this week about what you may have missed because of the time and energy you've dedicated to trivial and empty things that leave you feeling unfulfilled. Stop obsessing over the way you look and ask God to give you purpose and fulfillment outside of your appearance. True freedom is found when you can sacrifice your life for God's will. It's not always comfortable, and it's definitely not easy, but it will break away all chains and provide that lasting fulfillment for which you've been searching.

KEY VERSES:
"Let your eyes look straight ahead; fix your gaze directly before you."
Proverbs 4:25

REFLECTION QUESTIONS:
+ Angel shares, "Freedom is found in the place where I lose my life for the sake of something greater. God has shown me that the more willing I am to get outside of my own life, the more I will find where true, full life abounds." What have you been missing because of the time you've spent trying to perfect your image? How can you stop obsessing over trying to perfect your own image and start focusing on reflecting the image of God?

DAY 4

Wake up. Roll over. Turn off alarm. Scroll through Instagram.

Many of us have been practicing this daily routine for years. We wake up in the morning and immediately start feeding our minds with snapshots from other people's highlight reels. Our messy hair, morning breath, and three-sizes-too-big t-shirt don't seem to measure up to the perfection we see on our screen. Comparison, envy, anxiety, and self-loathing immediately set in whether we're aware of it or not. We begin another day knee-deep in the comparison cycle. But let's imagine a different reality for a moment.

Wake up. Roll over. Turn off alarm. Open Bible.

Starting with the Word of God as your daily routine and feeding your mind with truth, purpose, and encouragement can drastically change your day and your thought life. You'll probably even start to love those moments with messy hair, morning breath, and your three-sizes-too-big t-shirt because those will be the times you'll feel the most loved, seen, and known by your Father in heaven. Create intentional rhythms and routines in your life during your time in college that will draw you close to the heart of God and keep you in sync with His voice.

KEY VERSES:
"Satisfy us in the morning with your unfailing love, that we may sing for joy and be glad all our days."
Psalm 90:14

REFLECTION QUESTIONS:
+ Is there anything in your life that you need to release because it is creating a cycle of comparison? How can you practically go to Jesus first, rather than social media or the mirror?